# A GAME of THRONES
## PUZZLE QUEST

**METRO BOOKS**
New York

An Imprint of Sterling Publishing
1166 Avenue of the Americas
New York, NY 10036

METRO BOOKS and the distinctive Metro Books logo are
trademarks of Sterling Publishing Co., Inc.

© 2014 by Carlton Books Limited
Illustrations © 2014 by Carlton Books Limited

ISBN 978-1-4351-5783-5

For information about custom editions, special sales, and premium
and corporate purchases, please contact Sterling Special Sales at
800-805-5489 or specialsales@sterlingpublishing.com.

Manufactured in China

2 4 6 8 10 9 7 5 3

www.sterlingpublishing.com

# A GAME of THRONES
## PUZZLE QUEST

RIDDLES, ENIGMAS AND QUIZZES
INSPIRED BY THE HIT TV SERIES
AND FANTASY NOVELS

TIM DEDOPULOS

METRO BOOKS
New York

# CONTENTS

# SUMMER

# FALL

## WINTER

# INTRODUCTION

Geore R. R. Martin began writing his masterwork political fantasy series *A Song of Ice and Fire* in 1991. Although the first novel, *A Game of Thrones*, was published to little acclaim in 1996, the series has gone on to take the world by storm. More than 24 million copies have been sold in America alone. The books draw much of their inspiration from medieval European history, including the British Wars of the Roses. The HBO television series based on the books, *Game of Thrones*, has likewise proved itself a world-beater.

One of the toughest parts of writing a puzzle book like this is balancing the needs of the problems with the sanctity of a much-loved setting. I've done my best to present an entertaining range of mental challenges without trampling all over GRRM's fabulous lore. The puzzles in this volume are set across the entire time range of the books, and I've done my best to ensure that nothing in here specifically contradicts *A Song of Ice and Fire*'s canon.

I've also tried to make sure that I don't have individuals behaving too badly out of character, or involved in things that would seem implausible. You're more likely to find that questions of tangled kinship involve Walder Frey's

brood than Daenerys Targaryen, for example. Where feasible, I've ascribed specialities to characters who remained somewhat uncertain – the teaching of mathematics, for example, I assigned to Archmaester Mollos, rather than Archmaester Walgrave – and placed invented characters in Houses that to date have been mentioned only in passing.

But don't worry about needing to have the novels memorized. Of all the puzzles in here, only the ten quizzes require a knowledge of the series. Everything else is readily solvable with a bit of logic, deduction and patience. Gauging the difficulty of puzzles is a tricky business – different minds find different things tough – but in general, each season's questions will be a little harder than those of the one before.

The most important thing, of course, is to have fun. Puzzle-solving is, like story-telling, one of the few recreational habits found in all human societies, from the most ancient right up to the present day. So put on your thinking head and dive in. Westeros (and beyond) awaits you!

Tim Dedopulos, London, 2014

Spring

# 1

# KIRRA'S APPLES

The peace of Cider Hall was ruffled when Kirra came stamping up to Ser Bryan, bristling with anger. "Ser Fossoway, that ape Tregard is out of order. I beg you, please speak to him."

Ser Bryan sighed. "What is it this time, woman?"

"I need to know how this week's apple-picking has been. How am I supposed to do my job otherwise? All he'll tell me is that if I take the number of barrels gathered, and then add to that a quarter of that number, I'd come to 15 barrels. What's wrong with the man?"

"He likes you."

How many barrels of apples are there?

**Solution on page 160**

# SQUARED SERS

er Manfryd Yew and Ser Raynard Ruttiger fell to conversation during a feast at Casterly Rock. To their astonishment, they discovered that they had more in common than just their liege lord.

Each had a wife, a son and a daughter. When added together, the ages of the Yews totalled 100 years – as did that of the Ruttigers. Furthermore, if each family member's age was squared, then the squared ages of wife, son and daughter added together equalled the father's squared age in both cases. The only difference was that Ser Manfryd's daughter was one year younger than her brother, while Ser Raynard's daughter was two years younger.

How old are the two knights and their families?

Solution on page 160

# FOWLER PLAY

Jeyne and Jennelyn Fowler were identical – slender and pretty, with wispy yellow hair. Prince Quentyn could never tell them apart, and today, they'd ensured that their outfits matched perfectly. As he approached, they favoured him with devilish smiles.

"Good day, Prince…"

"…Quentyn. We hope…"

"…you are well."

Quentyn bowed nervously. "Ladies."

"Oh no, that…"

"…won't do…"

"…at all. Surely…"

"…you know us?"

"I am Jeyne, am I not?" said the one on the left.

"I am Jennelyn, am I not?" said the one on the right.

Before Quentyn could reply, Ferne, their lady in waiting, leaned forward to whisper in his ear. "One of them is lying, my lord. I swear this to be true."

Which is which?

Solution on page 161

# OLD WYK

**D**uring the years of preparation before being given to the sea a second time, acolytes of the Drowned God must train, learn and be purified. Their keep stands on the shores of Nagga's Cradle, a tall, grey building as stern as the sea itself.

New acolytes were housed in a square block broken into a three-by-three grid of cells, three acolytes to a cell. The central cell held the master of the dormitory, Cerron, an old, blind Drowned Man. The years weighed heavily on him but he retained wits enough to remember that so long as each side of the dormitory held nine acolytes, all was well.

It did not take the 24 acolytes long to realize that Cerron could be fooled. It proved simple to arrange themselves so that a full quarter of their number could slip away from the dormitory to drink and gossip on the shores of the bay.

How did they do it?

Solution on page 161

# THE MAESTER'S HAND

"You, boy. Roone. Hold your right palm in front of your mouth and blow slowly onto it."

"Maester?"

"Just do it, boy. There. How does it feel?"

"Damp, Maester, and warm."

"Quite right. Now, replace your right palm with your left, purse your lips, and blow on it strongly. Come on, quickly. How does that feel?"

"Cool, Maester."

"Just so. Why?"

Solution on page 162

# 6

# DRAGONSTONE

On the island of Dragonstone, hidden deep below the dungeons of the Stone Drum, an ancient Targayen tomb was carved into the living obsidian of Dragonmont. Within it lie two husbands with their two wives, two fathers with their two daughters, two grandmothers with their two granddaughters, two mothers with their two sons, two sisters with their two brothers, and two girls with their two mothers. Just six names are given, one for each inhabitant.

How is this possible?

Solution on page 163

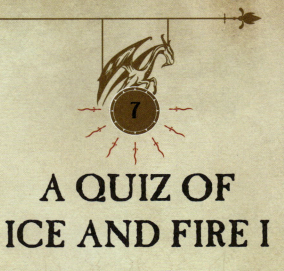

# A QUIZ OF ICE AND FIRE I

1. Who helps Robb Stark save his brother Bran from wildlings?

2. What was the name of Tyrion Lannister's first wife?

3. Which exiled knight enters service with Viserys and Daenerys Targaryen in Essos?

4. How did Davos Seaworth save Storm's End from starvation?

5. Which character in the *Game of Thrones* TV show does Emilia Clarke play?

6. What is the name of the ancestral castle of House Tully?

7. Who is Sansa Stark married to?

8. Who exposes Arya Stark's identity to the Brotherhood Without Banners?

9. To whom do House Swyft owe allegiance?

10. What is the name of the assassin who agrees to kill three victims for Arya Stark?

Solution on page 164

# LORD DAERON VAITH

Lord Daeron Vaith of the Red Dunes glared at the three men in front of him. The dock workers had been squabbling for some days now, and it had escalated to the point where the feud was becoming problematic. He was tempted to punish all three, but capriciousness was a last resort.

Stripped down to their barest bones and freed of the assorted accusations and counter claims, the arguments of the three men could be summarized as follows:

Gage: Alarn is lying.

Alarn: Rafe is lying.

Rafe: Both Gage and Alarn are lying.

Which man is telling the truth?

Solution on page 165

**9**

# VARYS

**M**y clothing's fine as velvet rare,

Though under earth my dwellings lie,

And when above it I appear,

My enemies do me decry.

The gardener's hate for me is fine,

I spoil his works as he does mine.

Who am I?

Solution on page 165

# FAIRMARKET

**B**uilt at the blue fork of the river Trident, Fairmarket is known throughout the Riverlands as a fine place for trading grain. Lumm, a trader by need more than by inclination, has a hundred bushels of high-quality barley, just eight percent chaff. To make it go further, his plan is to swap it for a larger quantity of cheaper barley, a third chaff, to then sell on in the city to those who don't know much better.

How many bushels of the cheaper barley would provide a fair exchange?

Solution on page 166

# HOUSE MARTELL

In the Water Gardens of Sunspear, four lesser knights of House Martell were sitting discussing events. After a time, talk turned to family and the nature of their various interrelationships.

Harlen turned to Selmont and said, "Petyr has the same relationship to Theodor as I do to you, you know."

Selmont nodded. "Yes. After all, you are to Theodor as Petyr is to you."

How are the men related?

Solution on page 166

# THE BAY OF CRABS

Daffyn and Whelan fell to arguing over who was faster on foot, and once coin was laid on the outcome, a proper race became inevitable. Jhon Mooton agreed to referee, picked a course along the shore of the Bay of Crabs a mile-and-a-half in length, and stationed people at the quarter-marks and at halfway.

When all was said and done, Daffyn won but by less than a full stride, and the two were neck-and-neck all the way. To general amazement, the first half of the race took exactly the same amount of time as the second half. The men hit the three-quarter point in six-and-three-quarters minutes, and it took as long from halfway to three-quarters as it did from the three-quarter mark to the end.

How long did the race take?

Solution on page 167

# A HUNT FOR WORDS I

```
R N N W O T S Y A W O R R A H
H E A R T E A T E R V Y J M R R
W V L N S H E L B Q L G N B H
E E A W O J G Y L I M Y Y E L
D S S W O E X R Q A O G T R L
Y E E K R F T N E O R E L L O
T H R G S W I J D E L I N Y R
K T E N N J R P S Y N E A V Q
C N S H I E L D K M L A N S A
A R E Y F N Y M E R I A W N M
L O D A F Y K H A D O K H A A
B B J F I A J F O R A X M K Y
N E F E R J Y H T N I L F E I
G R I G G Q N U G V U Y Q S X
S T K G S A R G O N I V A C M
```

| | | |
|---|---|---|
| AENYS | HARROWAYS TOWN | OLENNA |
| AMBERLY | HEARTEATER | ORELL |
| BLACKTYDE | JAFER | QAMAYI |
| FARLEN | JAYNE | RHLLOR |
| FLINT | JINQI | ROBERT |
| FOWLER | KHADOKH | SARGON |
| GERGEN | KHEWO | SHIELD |
| GREENAWAY | MARIYA | SNAKES |
| GRIFFINS ROOST | NEFER | TALLA |
| GRIGG | NYMERIA | THE SEVEN |

Solution on page 168

# 14

# DORNISH TROUBLE

Lord Varner had urgent business with House Qorgyle, in the Dornish deserts, so he sent his man Abelarn to castle Sandstone to open discussions. The road past the Hellholt is long and murderously hot at times and Abelarn found the journey increasingly difficult.

Four days out from Sandstone, he knew that he needed to find a specific place of shelter that night. If he travelled at 10 miles per hour, he'd pass the shelter a full hour after sunset and risk missing it altogether. If he travelled at 15 miles per hour, he'd arrive an hour before sunset and would have to sit in the heat, without even the faint breeze of his riding to cool him.

What speed does he need to travel to arrive exactly at sunset?

Solution on page 169

# 15

# CHICKENS

A group of White Harbor men are meeting with a livestock merchant with the intention of buying a consignment of live chickens. Having negotiated a price that all concerned find acceptable, the men find that they have a problem dividing the cost amongst themselves evenly. If each of them pays nine pennies, they will be paying 11 pennies too much, but if each puts in six, then they have 16 pennies too little.

How many buyers are there, and what is the cost of their chickens?

Solution on page 170

# FIRST IMPRESSIONS

**D**o you have the wit to see,

Ragged though our mien might be,

A hint of glitter in our veins?

Grind off dust and gold remains.

Often sought by men are we,

None who know us can disagree.

So tell me then – who are we?

# A LESSON OVER DINNER

Archmaester Mollos waved his red gold rod at the novices waiting nervously in front of him and grunted disapprovingly. "You dolts seem determined to resist learning even the simplest application of numbers. So this afternoon, I have decided to give you some... encouragement.

It is my estimate that you typically manage to consume 20 spoons of food at your evening meal. Tonight, your portions will depend on your wits. The five of you will get your 100 spoons – rabbit stew, I believe it is tonight – but they will not be shared equally. The amount of food each of you gets will be staggered, decreasing by the same amount each time. The two smallest shares together will equal just one-seventh of the three collected larger shares. The first of you to tell me how many spoons each share contains will get the largest portion. The last of you will receive the smallest and I warn you now, it isn't much. Fail, and go without."

What size are the shares?

Solution on page 171

# FREY TIME

For one long summer, Arwyn Frey found herself placed in a strange and difficult position. Her mother Annara took her to a small manor and left her in the care of her aunt and uncle, with strict instructions to obey them in all particulars. None of her cousins were in attendance.

She was given a haircut and ordered to keep away from one entire wing. Most of the time, she was left to her own devices and her aunt and uncle were distant, at best. At other times, she was instructed to put on specific sets of clothing, sit in very precise locations in the manor and engage in various trivial pursuits with her aunt and uncle. During these periods, and these periods alone, they were extremely pleasant and sociable.

Strange noises from the forbidden wing led Arwyn to suspect that the manor was haunted, although her uncle Errik was particularly curt regarding that possibility. He was less reticent about a fellow who appeared to stalk the grounds of the manor, owning him to be a dangerous lunatic. Even so, Ser Errik made no attempt to run the man off.

Eventually, after some weeks of this, Arwyn was sent home, none the wiser.

What was going on?

Solution on page 172

# LISKER'S TASK

"**S**uppose, young Lisker, that there are 15 novices, yourself included."

"Yes, Archmaester."

"Further imagine that there is a task I have that requires a group of three novices. If I order you to change the members of your group each hour, and to progress at the task for seven hours without ever repeating the members of your group, is that possible?"

Solution on page 172

# THUNDERFIST

Tormund Tall-Talker, Father of Hosts, took his title very literally. Somewhere between 50 and 80 years old, he was known to boast to have as many sons and grandsons as he had years of life. Each of his sons, so he said, had as many sons as brothers.

How old was he?

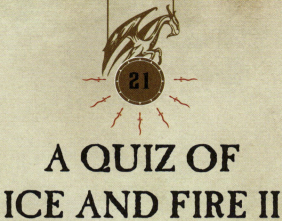

# A QUIZ OF
# ICE AND FIRE II

1.   What is Jon Snow's first assignment on the Wall?

2.   Who is the master-of-arms at Castle Black when Jon Snow arrives?

3.   Why is Sansa Stark's direwolf "Lady" killed?

4.   Who portrays Khal Drogo in the Game of Thrones TV show?

5.   Which city is the first to welcome Daenerys as The Mother Of Dragons?

6.   What is the name of Theon Greyjoy's first ship?

7.   Which Lord is known as the Old Man of Oldtown?

8.   Who does Tywin Baratheon plan to have married to the Lord of Flowers?

9.   What is the identity of Theon Greyjoy's torturer?

10.  Who said "There are no true knights, no more than there are gods"?

Solution on page 174

# DAENERYS'S TEA

**T**he Braavosi maid knelt at Daenerys's feet and held up a silver tray. "Spiceflower and cinnamon tea, m'lady. There is honey to sweeten, if you like."

"Thank you." Daenerys took the cup, and sipped. Suppressing a grimace, she swiftly spooned in enough honey to make it palatable. She drank again. "Pleasant." She set the cup on the table and was about to return to her discussion when a large beetle flew past her clumsily and splashed straight into the tea.

The maid gasped and snatched the cup back. "I'm so sorry, m'lady. I will bring you more tea." She bowed again, and vanished.

A little while later, the maid returned with a fresh tea. Daernerys took a sip and frowned at the maid. "Is it your usual custom to lie to your master's guests?"

How did she know it was the same cup of tea?

Solution on page 175

# DAYNE'S PARADOX

**S**er Dayne smiled at Arya Stark. "I heard that you've said my fellow Dornishmen are liars, young lady. Well, let me tell you true: all Dornishmen are indeed constant liars."

"How do I know you're telling the truth?" Arya said, suspicious.

"If I'm telling you the truth then clearly I have to be lying. But if I'm lying then I'm just confirming the truth."

"It doesn't work like that," she protested.

"Oh?" Ser Dayne smiled. "How does it work then?"

Can you explain?

# THE SPRAWLING

**E**mblem of youth and innocence,

With walls surrounded for defence,

Yet by no worldly cares oppressed,

I boldly spread my charms around,

Till some rude lover breaks the mound,

And rudely clasps me to his breast.

Here soon I sicken and decay

My beauty lost, I'm turned away.

Who am I?

Solution on page 176

# 25

# A CAUTIOUS PACE

**S**ent by the Brotherhood on an errand, Thoros of Myr took his time on the outward journey, ambling along at a rate of four miles an hour. On his return, keen to be done with it all, he stirred himself to a more respectable six miles an hour.

What was his average speed?

## 26

# A MATTER OF BIRTHDAYS

"**G**ood evening, Ser Andar."

"Maester Hakon! It's an honour to see you here at Runestone this evening."

"Thank you, Ser. It is good to see you well. How many are you expecting at this gathering?"

"I believe there will be 23 of us."

"Twenty-three. That is a most interesting number. I wonder if you know the chance, at a gathering of 23, that two of those present will have been born on the same day of the year?"

"Ah…"

What's the chance?

Solution on page 177

# A HUNT FOR WORDS II

```
M R Q A J B B A R C E L Z G R
L S R E W O T E E R H T N O F
E S H A D D N M A H O O Y Y F
N A G G S E N O T S I R T L S
N R Y M I R H N S A P R G E E
O Y E G E A M D R Q L H R E A
D A M M E J H A I R Y E S T S
C W K D A T H Q F X N N A S M
S A Y L E N R A A A S S N Q O
R A V G O A D Y H F O S V O K
J Y R E V O C O O A C Q I R E
N L L Y D N A R N L U U L G G
W I L L E M L E K Y L A R Y S
R O N I L E A Q C S X R L L M
F I J Y Y U U X J E C E X E V
```

| | | |
|---|---|---|
| AELINOR | HAIGH | QORGYLE |
| AEMOND | HAIRY | RANDYLL |
| ALVYN | HOARE | RORGE |
| ANVIL | JARED | SARYA |
| COVER | JAYDE | SEA SMOKE |
| CRABB | JONOS | SHADD |
| DONNEL | KDATH | STEELY |
| EDMYN | LARYS | TALEA |
| ELYAS | LUCOS | THREE TOWERS |
| ERENA | MAEGE | TORRHEN'S SQUARE |
| FALYSE | MANDON | TRISTON |
| FIRST | MEJHAH | WILLEM |
| FORLEY | OLYVAR | |
| GOADY | PRYOR | |

Solution on page 178

# 28

# AGE OF AMBROSE

"So you see, Ser Jason, in seven years time, my and Alyssane's combined ages will be 64 years."

"Arthur is quite right, Lord Mallister. When he were the age that I am now, he was twice as old as I was then."

What ages are the Ambroses?

Solution on page 179

## 29

# THE MALLISTERS

"Fascinating, Ser Arthur. Alys and I also have an interesting confluence of our ages, as it happens. Her age and mine use the same numbers, but reversed, and the difference between our ages is but an eleventh of their total."

"I am definitely younger than Jason however, Lord Ambrose."

What ages are the Mallisters?

Solution on page 179

# TANNER

**W**attle had been apprenticed to Maise the Tanner for six months. Even by the high standards of Reeking Lane, tanning was a foul and dangerous business but the lad was keen to make a good impression. Dunking skins into an acid bath one afternoon, and watching the level of the liquid rise within its tub, he found himself wondering if it might not be possible to save money. Anything that meant using less acid would be an improvement in his life, as well.

A much wider rod, he reasoned, would take up more space in the bath, so the acid would rise higher and treat more of the skin lashed to it. Then, of course, he realized that the bath would need to be higher, to stop the acid spilling. But the rods would be taking up space there as well and the acid would rise higher still, and if he made the bath higher yet, the rods would still be there, and no matter how high he made the tub…

He shuddered as, in his imagination, cascades of acid flooded out of a towering bath and stripped the very flesh from his bones. Was he right to be concerned?

Solution on page 180

# THREE BOXES

**A**rchmaester Mollos placed three small boxes on the table before him, and looked up at the novices assembled before him. "Three boxes," he declared. "Each one holds two small bags and each bag contains a single coin. In one box, there are two gold dragons. In another, two silver stags. In the third, one dragon and one stag. I do not remember which box holds which coins. You, Hobb, come here, and take a bag from one of the boxes."

Nervously, the novice did as he was told.

"Good. Now, what coin is inside?"

Hobb opened the bag. "A dragon, sir."

"Fine. Now, which of you dolts can tell me what the chance is that the other coin in that same box is also a gold dragon?"

Solution on page 180

## SER GLADDEN

"Ser Gladden, how old are you?"

"A bold question, child. In six years time, I will be one-and-a-quarter the age I was four years ago."

How old is Ser Gladden?

Solution on page 181

# 33

# THE WOODSMAN

**W**hen three farms were robbed in as many days by a tall, muscular, weathered-looking fellow with a big nose and a huge beard, the House Leygood guards were immediately suspicious that the beard had been used as a way of throwing them off the villain's trail. After a little investigation, they found a heap of trimmed facial hair not far from the third victim's home.

Suspicion fell on a local woodsman, named Crom. He was of the right build, depth of tan and nasal prominence, and was now clean-shaven, despite several villagers remembering him as being bearded six months before. He insisted that he was innocent and that he had removed his beard four months prior, following a nasty incident with woodlice, a bottle of spirits and an open bonfire.

Sentiment quickly turned against him, however, and it was looking bleak until a Leygood guardsman with more wits than usual pointed out an element of Crom's appearance that ruled him out beyond any doubt. What was it?

Solution on page 182

# SIX BARRELS

The landlord of the Inn at the Crossroads, Masha Heddle, purchased six barrels of unusually good wine from a vintner. One was of a vintage significantly better than the rest and that she kept for herself. The others, still sealed, went to two customers, one of whom bought twice as many pints of wine as the other. Each barrel held a different amount and their sizes were 15 pints, 16 pints, 18 pints, 19 pints, 20 pints and 31 pints.

Which barrel was the one that Masha kept for herself?

# Summer

# GERIS CHARLTON

**G**eris Charlton was often heard to boast that he had twice as many sisters as brothers, while his twin sister Gerra had just as many brothers as sisters. Eventually, his aunt Berenia pointed out that his cousin Leystone had three times as many sisters as brothers, while Leystone's sister Rhee still had just as many brothers as sisters.

Who had the more brothers, Geris or Leystone?

Solution on page 183

# A TRAY OF CAKES

At Winterfell, Gage had baked three batches of apple cakes. Each batch was slightly different – the first had added blueberries, the second contained pine-nuts and the third featured chopped prunes. When the batches were finished, he put them aside carefully, in the order of their cooking, so he'd know which was which.

To his annoyance, when he returned to the apple cakes, one of the other cooks had shifted the platters around so that none of them were in the correct position. Given his reluctance to waste his work, what is the fewest number of apple cakes he would have to cut open to find out the identities of each platter?

# BUTTERWELL

"Family relationships can swiftly get tangled, even in the Riverlands. Perla is Shay's third cousin once removed, on her mother's side. What relation is Perla's grandmother to Shay's son?

Solution on page 184

# INFINITE REALMS

"**P**lay close attention to this, Frey."

"Yes, Archmaester Mollos."

"Start with a number and add one to it. How far can you keep going, getting ever-larger numbers?"

"Forever, sir."

"Quite. Now, start with the same original number and add two to it. Again how far can you keep going?"

"Well, it would be forever again."

"Exactly. So riddle me this, young Robert. Collect up all the numbers you count, in both those sequences. Which of the sequences is larger?"

Solution on page 185

# A QUIZ OF
# ICE AND FIRE III

1.  Why does Ned Stark try to resign as Hand of the King?

2.  Who is known as The Spider?

3.  What is odd about the raven in Bran Stark's dreams?

4.  Alfie Allen, who plays Theon Greyjoy in the Game of Thrones TV show is the brother of which musical artist?

5.  Who leads the defence of the Mud Gate at the battle of Blackwater?

6.  Who is named Savior of King's Landing?

7.  Who leads the Faith of the Seven?

8.  How did Maester Qyburn lose his chain?

9.  How does Lord Rickard Karstark die?

10. What is Hag's Teeth?

Solution on page 186

# DAARIO AND THE GREY WORM

Daario Naharis and the Grey Worm found themselves in so heated an argument that the Worm was in danger of considering raising his voice a little – and all over the matter of a game.

"You're being a blind, obstinate fool," Daario yelled. He made a Herculean effort to calm himself. "It is clearly easier to roll at least three sixes from 18 dice-tosses than it is to get at least one six from six tosses. There are so many more chances."

The Grey Worm shook his head politely. "You are incorrect. It is the other way around."

Who is correct?

Solution on page 187

# KHALEESI OF THORNS

"What has Lady Olenna got for us today?"

"She wants to walk down to the Mander," Arryk said.

Erryk sighed. "Walk? Gods, why?"

"Who knows? Watch the boats, maybe."

"It'll take an age. Three miles an hour downhill to get there maybe, but one mile an hour back uphill."

"You had something else to do with those six hours?" asked Arryk. "It's not as if we have to jog."

"I suppose not."

Lady Olenna's screech came from the other room. "Left! Right! Come here."

"Here we go again," Erryk said.

How far is the journey?

Solution on page 187

# A HUNT FOR WORDS III

```
M A E R I E S M A R W Y L L A
A Y J D L T E K E L R U K A A
C C L D J V A R D I S N R N D
O Y J E G D U M E F K K Y O O
R X Y D S T E P C N U A W D O
N N Z N L R E B M O L I O H W
E D M U N D N L A N L Y L A N
E S V O B O M M U L P P L D O
T Y Z S D N N S F C L D I N R
A E N A R R K O U L A E W A Y
E L L O C K E L T O S Y R D
R E H T A E W Y R R E M E R B
G M S L T O R G O N A L Y U D
N E B B I K N Y W E L M C R P
N A M O W G N I P E E W F W K
```

ACORN
AENAR
BLACK
CLETUS
DONAL
EDMUND
ELADON
ELLERY
GREAT
IBBEN
JEYNE
KURLEKET
LAYNA
LEWYN

LOCKE
LUCAS
MAERIE
MARLON
MELEYS
MERRYWEATHER
MUDGE
MYLES
NESTOR
OMBER
PLUMM
RANDA
RENLY
RYELLA

RYMOLF
SKULL
SOUND
TORGON
VARDIS
VULTURE
WALDA
WEEPING WOMAN
WILLOW
WYLLA
YRONWOOD
YUNKAI

Solution on page 188

# QARTH

**X**aro Xhoan Daxos turned the parchment over thoughtfully. It had been delivered by a slave but bore no identifying signature or seal. The message was short, and if it was a threat then it was a particularly oblique and subtle one.

In a beautiful, flowing hand, the message read, "A stack and its seventh together reach 19."

There was nothing more. Try as he might, Xaro could discern no purpose in the message.

How big is the stack?

Solution on page 189

# TWO TWINS

Two twins we are and there is no surprise,

That we're alike in feature, shape, and size.

We're often round, of brass or iron made,

Or mayhaps wood, yet useful still in trade.

But even so, for all our daily pains,

We by the neck are often hung in chains.

What are we?

Solution on page 190

# BRIDGER CERWYN

"**D**id you hear, Andar? When Lord Medger's father, Bridger Cerwyn, married his current wife, 18 years ago, he was three times as old as Beedie, his bride."

"So what?"

"So now, he's just twice as old as she is."

"Well how old was he, then, when they married?"

Solution on page 190

# MEN WITHOUT HATS

Three separate men were sitting in the Red Dome coffee house in central Braavos. The first, Gergen, was cautiously watching the door. The second, Barth, was just as cautiously watching Gergen. The third, Mudge, was being even more careful about watching Barth. One of the things that Barth noted was that Gergen had long, slightly greasy hair that held a faint scent of offal. Mudge, unobserved as he was by either man, was as hairlessly bald as it was possible for a man to become.

Given that Barth's baldness or hairiness was unrecorded, can you tell whether, amongst the three, there was a bald man looking at a hairy man?

Solution on page 191

# THE GREAT OTHER

A small stir arose in the Temple of the Lord of Light in Volantis when a long-forgotten prophecy attributed to a priest of the Great Other was discovered on Crackclaw Point. The prophecy warned that a circle of adepts of the Great Other should be maintained at all times, lest ruin result. The priests of R'hllor immediately started working to uncover the full import of the scroll.

One of the prophecy's clearer sections described the number that had to form the circle – seven blind, to see behind the light; three blind in one eye, to see both light and shade; five with normal vision, to perceive the truth; and nine who see through one eye, for focus and purity.

What are the maximum and minimum sizes of the circle of adepts?

Solution on page 191

# VALAR MORGHULIS

Ser Normon Wythers was in his library, working. His wife, Cerenda, was in her own rooms in the keep when she heard raised voices from the library. Her husband, sounding concerned, was talking to an angry-sounding man with a rough voice. She couldn't make out the words, but the argument intensified until she heard a horrible scream, followed by a nasty thud, and silence.

Cerenda was already standing at the library door and trying it nervously, found it locked. Her screams fetched guards, who battered the door down and found Ser Norman dead, with a plain-looking dagger through his heart. The library windows were high above the ground but even so, they were intact and tightly latched on the inside. There were no other ways in or out of the room and no place where an intruder could have remained hidden.

Lady Cerenda admitted that her husband had been preoccupied for several weeks but he had given her no reason to believe that he was in danger. A maester was called and he was able to state with confidence that there was no supernatural element involved in Ser Normon's fate.

So what happened?

Solution on page 192

# PLAYING THE FIELD

**B**raganthos Woodwright was set upon making a grand gesture to impress Margaery Tyrell and he hit upon the idea of a very particular field. His plan was to make an enclosure for jousting and archery but to elevate it above all other fields, it would be perfectly square and surrounded by a barred wooden fence. The fence would be seven bars high at all points, to honour the gods, and would surround an area of exactly as many acres as there were bars. The wooden bars he selected for this endeavour were each 2.75 yards in length. For reference, you should probably know than one acre is 4,840 square yards, which you could consider as being equivalent to 55 x 88 yards.

What size will the field be?

Solution on page 193

# ALLYCE & WILLIT

"Ha ha, Willitt. I was behind you!"

"No way, Rolf. I was behind you!"

"No! I'm right!"

"No you're not! I'm right!"

Allyce sighed. "Quiet down, you two. You're both right."

How?

**51**

# THE PLANK

As Wat watched, his master, Desmon, sawed a thick plank into chunks. First of all, he sawed it precisely in half, then he fastened the pieces together and sawed them both in half. Finally, he gathered up all four chunks, and sawed them in half once more. Wiping dust off himself, Desmon grabbed one of the small pieces of wood, and tossed it across to Wat.

Wat looked at it doubtfully. "That was a 20-pound plank." Desmon nodded.

"So this weighs, uh, two-and-a-half pounds," said Wat.

Desmon spat on the floor. "Nope."

Where has Wat gone wrong?

Solution on page 194

# LAZY LEO

Acolyte Tyrell was somewhat startled when he rounded a corner in the Citadel to find Archmaester Mollos just standing there in front of him. He was even more startled when Mollos flourished a pair of envelopes at him. A hoarse "Sir?" was the best he could manage.

The old man glared at him. "One of these envelopes, acolyte, contains a credit slip for one silver stag. The other contains a slip for two silver stags. Pick one."

"Uh…"

"Pick one, or receive none, acolyte."

Tyrell snatched one hastily.

"So. This remaining envelope either has half as much value as the one you've chosen, or twice as much. You may exchange the one you have. Does it make sense to swap?"

Thinking furiously, Tyrell said, "Well, if I make the wrong choice I only lose half, but if I make the right choice, I gain the same again. That means the potential profit is double the potential risk. So yes, it makes sense."

"Very well," said Mollos. He swapped Tyrell's envelope. "Now, I ask you the same question. Does it make sense to swap?"

Tyrell's face fell. "Well yes… Ah."

What is wrong with his logic?

Solution on page 194

# A HUNDRED GEMS

"In Pentos, Illyrio came into a consignment of opals, which he decided to convert into livestock. He called one of his bronze-collared servants and gave the man 100 gems, with strict instructions to exchange them entirely for exactly 100 animals. The beasts he wanted were camels, at five opals each, asses at one opal each, and goats at 20 per opal, and at least one of each.

How many of each animal did the servant return with?

Solution on page 195

# PEARLS OF WISDOM

"Look at this pair of bags, novice. There is an identically sized stone in each bag, in each case either a bead or a pearl, with an even chance of each. Between them, the bags may hold two beads, two pearls, or one of each. Now, this pearl goes into the second bag, which is refastened. Pay attention. I shake that bag, and draw out... a pearl. So be it. Now both bags hold one stone again. Which bag – if either – is now more likely to be holding a pearl?"

Solution on page 195

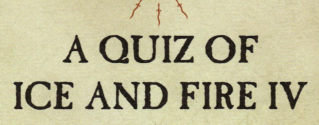

# A QUIZ OF
# ICE AND FIRE IV

1. What title does Robb Stark claim when the North secedes from the Seven Kingdoms?

2. What document does Cersei Lannister tear up before ordering Ned Stark arrested?

3. Where does King Robert Baratheon appoint Ned Stark as his Hand?

4. Who does Aidan Gillen play in the *Game of Thrones* TV show?

5. What is Mance Rayder's title?

6. Who orders Davos Seaworth to denounce Cersei's children as illegitimate to the whole of the Seven Kingdoms?

7. Where are the best far-eyes made?

8. What price does Daenerys Targaryen pay for the Unsullied?

9. What is Ser Brynden Tully's nickname?

10. Who had a horse called Glory?

Solution on page 196

# AS THE RAVEN FLIES

Travelling from Longtable to Ashford, it is possible to get diverted by heading instead to Cider Hall and from there completing your journey. Cider Hall is nearer to Longtable than Ashford is but it sits 12 miles from the road to Ashford. That indirect route is 35 miles. If all the roads are straight, how far is the direct route from Longtable to Ashford?

Solution on page 197

# GOLD AND GREEN

Ser Dunstad Westbrook was a fair man by nature. So when he was called on to adjudicate the terms of a rather obscure will left by a wealthy merchant, he was determined to do his best.

The deceased man wanted his sons to have gold squares commemorating their father. The gold square of the younger son had to have sides three-quarters the length of the square going to the elder son. For this purpose, the man had set aside enough gold to cover 100 square inches, at an even thickness of ¼-inch".

The issue that nobody could quite seem to settle on was the size of the two squares. How long should their sides be?

Solution on page 198

# THE DAWN'S DELAY

**I** was here before the world began, and shall forever last.

Born before the rivers ran, in dim and distant past.

Your youthful moments I attend and mitigate your grief;

The industrious peasant I befriend, and to victims bring relief.

Make much of me if you are wise and use me while you may,

For you will find that in a trice, you too I'll come to slay.

Who am I?

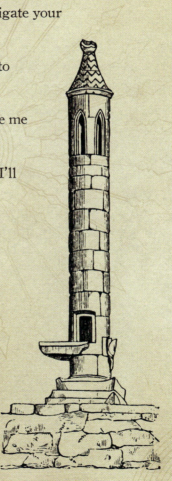

Solution on page 198

# REDFORT

Finding them together in a quiet moment, young Mychel darted up to his parents. "How old are you, mother?"

Lady Houtella blinked at the sudden interruption. "If you add your age, and mine, and your father's, it comes to precisely 70 years, with no months left over."

"That's a lot," said Mychel. "And how old are you, father?"

"Six times your age," said Lord Horton.

Mychel frowned. "So when will I be just half your age, then?"

"When that happens, our three ages will be double the total that they are today."

"But…"

"But now it's time for bed," Lady Houtella said firmly.

How old are the Redforts?

Solution on page 199

# RAYDER'S TOWER

**V**al the wildling came to the defence of a pair of children who'd offended the wildling warlord Mance Rayder, and almost before she knew it, she found herself locked with them in a tower of punishment, out in the deep woods. The tower was ice-clad, and nigh-impossible to climb, but it did have a pair of baskets linked by a pulley so that food could be provided. Getting into a basket without a strong counterweight would be disastrous – a 15lb disparity between basket loads was the most that a human could risk if trying to travel in a basket. She weighed a muscular 175lb, while Stig and Ynga weighed 95lb and 80lb respectively. After some thought, she made a big bundle of the fuel, food, water and furs in their cell, along with some chunks of hearthstone. When the bundle reached 65lb, she declared herself satisfied, and proceeded to get herself and the children down from the tower.

How?

Solution on page 200

# FAIR ISLE

**S**er Gareth Clifton was very particular about his will. Amongst his many bequests, he was particularly concerned about his wine cellar, which he wanted to share evenly amongst his five sons. He had 45 casks of fine wine that he wished to see distributed. Nine of them held four gallons, nine more held three gallons, a further nine held two gallons, another nine held one gallon, and the final nine were empty five-galloners, but still of value as well-seasoned casks.

How can he make sure that each son gets an identical volume of wine (18 gallons) and number of casks (nine), while still receiving at least one of each volume of cask?

Solution on page 201

## 62

# LADIES, NOT IN WAITING

**W**hen he entered the ballroom of the Red Keep, Tytos immediately noticed a group of lovely ladies talking together at a nearby table, including a couple of his acquaintance. Putting on his most charming smile, he sauntered over to them, and grandly declared, "Ten pretty maids, all in a row! By the Gods, I never did think to see such beauty."

Lady Marissa arched her eyebrow. "I'm afraid you seem to be badly mistaken, Ser Tytos. I'm afraid we are neither in a row, nor ten in number. However, I do suppose that if we were twice as many again as we are, we would of necessity be as far above ten so gathered as we presently are below it."

"Ug," Tytos said, thoroughly taken aback. "Um, thank you." With that he left, trying to ignore the giggles coming from behind him.

How many women are in the group?

Solution on page 201

# SER ONDRE

Ser Ondre had sent the new recruits to the Hellholt House Guard on a training run — 15 miles through the Dornish desert, with just one flask of water (and no resupply allowed), departing an hour before noon. First man back would win lighter duties for a week.

As Arrone fought his way back to the keep, throat as dry as the dust he was caked in, he saw another man sitting on the ground. Enrike looked dreadful, pale and panting, drenched in sweat. Ser Ondre stood over him, sternly. As Enrike finally caught his breath, Ser Ondre unleashed a torrent of the most hideously vile abuse at him, concluding with a month of punishment detail.

Arrone flinched as Ser Ondre turned to him, but the man merely nodded, and told him to go get refreshed.

What had Enrike done wrong?

# A HUNT FOR WORDS IV

```
C I L E W R Y V R C H T A A S
M A W L L I H R E V L I S S W
I A R E R Y L E S E U E H O K
G L T C N E L L A I R O O S E
O S L R O D D E N L R D Y S T
W Y V Y I S E R S E S C R H T
E W F J R C A L A D M W G P E
N L Z E K I E Y H L J I O A R
A E B A K E O E S A L R T R V
R M A E T C A S A D O A S S D
U Q E A N W I G M Y R P E T E
A L L I S Y T R B A E Y R A L
F S A M O L A E L F N P O N D
T O O F G N I D D U P S F I O
H O S T E E N S L Y N T E N N
```

ALLARD
ARSTAN
AURANE
BAELA
CARCOSA
CLEOS
DAYNE
ELDON
ESGRED
FOREST
GOWEN
HOSTEEN
ILLYRIOS MANSE
KETTER

LIGHT
LOMAS
LOREN
MASHA
MATRICE
MELWYS
NELLA
PUDDINGFOOT
PYPAR
RODDEN
ROOSE
RYLES
SAATH
SANSA

SHORE
SILVERHILL
SLATE
SLYNT
SWORD
ULRICK
UMBER
VEILED LADY
VYRWEL
WENDEL
WOODS
YSILLA

# A FOOL'S GAME

"**M**aester Lomys! Maester Lomys!"

Lomys turned to see Highgarden's fool, Butterbumps, bearing down on him. He shuddered lightly. "What is it?"

The fool grinned. "I have a game for you, Maester."

"I hardly think…"

"Oh, but you'll like this. I have collected a basket of 50 potatoes. I will lay them out in a straight line, increasingly far apart. The first two are just one yard from each other. The third is three yards from the second. The fourth is five yards from the third. And so on. Your part is to collect them again, one at a time, and gather them in a heap by the first potato."

Lomys stared at the jester coldly. "I can hardly accuse you of having lost your wits, given that foolishness and flatulence comprise your entire purpose, but you'll have to search elsewhere for victims. Perhaps Ser Vortimer can lend you a dullard to torment. Shoo. Bedevil someone else."

How far would Lomys have to walk to collect the fool's potatoes?

Solution on page 204

# BREA'S FEAST

**B**rea the cook watched Maester Tallan twitch nervously, and mutter to himself. Eventually, she went over to him to find out was ailing the old fellow.

"A troublesome dinner to arrange, mistress Brea," the man replied.

"No matter to me," she assured him. "However many as is coming, I'll feed 'em."

"I'm sure, I'm sure," Tallan said. "But the protocol! Ser Buford is hosting his brother's father-in-law, his father-in-law's brother, his father's brother-in-law and his brother-in-law's father."

"What of it?" asked Brea, mystified. "It's just four guests."

Maester Tallen threw his hands in the air. "No, no! That would be the most Ser Buford could be expecting. But he has invited just the very least!"

Brea frowned. "How many is that, then?"

Solution on page 204

# GOODBROOK

When Ser Goodbrook died, his will instructed that his eldest son should receive half of his beloved herd of stallions. One-third of the herd was to go to the middle son, and one-ninth to the youngest. Unfortunately, at that time, Ser Goodbrook's herd numbered 17 horses, and his sons could see no way to divide the herd up as requested without dividing one or more horses into bloody chunks.

When they discussed the matter with the stable master, he was able to fix the matter – at no personal loss to himself – so that it was possible to share the herd fairly between the brothers without killing any horses, and without involving any fifth parties.

How can this be done?

Solution on page 205

# SIMEON STAR-EYES

"They say that Symeon Star-Eyes was so skilled that given a target 40 feet away, he could fire an arrow straight through his hat every time he tried."

"They do, do they? That's not difficult, you fool. Give me a minute with old Blind Pew and I'll have him doing the same ten times in a row."

"Nonsense. Old Pew hasn't held a bow in 30 years and even then he couldn't hit a chicken in a henyard. Star-Eyes was a mighty hero!"

"A gold dragon says I'm right."

What's the way to do it?

**69**

# BAQQ

The Windblown known as Beans was fond of dice, and during a dull hour at the siege of Astapor he concocted a new game to inflict upon his comrades. Taking a board, he divided it into six sections and numbered them from one to six. Then he invited his friends to bet on a particular number to come up on the throw of three dice. Anyone who picked a number that showed on any of the three dice would get their stake back, plus the same again for each dice that showed that number. So, for example, betting on 'four' for a roll of four, two, four would return your original wager, plus twice as much again.

As a player, what is the chance of winning at this game?

Solution on page 207

# THE DOOR'S GUARD

**W**hat force and strength cannot get through,

I with a gentle touch can do,

And many in the streets would stand,

Were I not right there at hand.

What am I?

Solution on page 207

# Fall

# A QUIZ OF ICE AND FIRE V

1. What is Viserys' golden crown?

2. Why does Tywin Lannister want his son Tyrion to serve as Hand of the King?

3. Why did Samwell Tarly take the Black?

4. Who does Kit Harrington play in the Game of Thrones TV show?

5. To where is Brienne of Tarth ordered to escort the imprisoned Jaime Lannister?

6. Who is the Spice King?

7. In which region are the Water Gardens?

8. Who helps Jon Snow defeat the wildling raider Orell?

9. What are Melisandre's plans for Robert Baratheon's bastard son Gendry?

10. What name is given to the bastard children of the Reach?

Solution on page 208

# 72

# KILLJOY

One particularly blustery day, when the wind was blowing a strong, steady easterly, it took the oarsmen of the Salty Wench just 90 minutes to cover the 24 miles from Pyke to Saltcliffe. The return journey more than made up for it however, taking an entire quarter-day.

How long would the round trip have taken in a dead calm?

Solution on page 209

# GOLD HONORS

In the comfort of the Merchant's House in Volantis, the traders Triorro, Nassicho and Donnimo were discussing a possible purchase of a consignment of spice. The price of the shipment was high, at 28 gold honors, and none of the men had enough gold honors on him to complete the purchase alone.

"If I borrowed half of the gold honors that you two hold, I could buy the spice," said Triorro.

"If I borrowed two-thirds of the gold honors that you two hold, then I could buy the spice," said Nassicho.

"And if I borrowed three-quarters of the gold honors that you two hold, I could buy the spice," said Donnimo.

How many gold honors does each trader have available?

# THE MUSTER

"Stilwood, assemble the boys."

"At once, Ser Gregor."

"Huh. Rows of five is no good, there's three left over. Try sevens."

"Rows of seven, gentlemen."

"What? Still two. What is this shit? What about threes?"

"Uh, of course, Ser Gregor. Rows of three, gents."

"No! Still two left over. Damn, this is making my head hurt. Stilwood, we're gonna have to kill a couple. Who's useless?"

What's the least number of men Ser Gregor is trying to muster?

Solution on page 210

## 75

# SALTSPEAR

Heading to Barrowtown, a trapper found himself needing to cross the Saltspear river with a dog, a drunkard and a case of wine. He could manage to ford the river easily enough with one of the three but the dog hated the drunkard and was desperate to savage him. Similarly, the drunkard was urgently attempting to get at the wine.

Cursing the idiocy of the Gods, the trapper set about trying to work out how to get all three across without losing one or more of them.

How did he do it?

Solution on page 210

# A RANGER'S DEATH

**W**alking through the Shadow Tower, Ser Denys Mallister discovered a ranger, Hale, in the throes of death. Noting someone nearby, Ser Denys approached and the man fled. When finally apprehended, the man turned out to be a recent recruit, named Weir. It was no secret that Hale had taken a dislike to Weir but the man was unarmed. Hale had been stabbed through the neck with something sharp and irregularly shaped but there was no knife or pick to be found, neither by the body nor anywhere along the corridor that Hale had fled down. Furthermore, Hale claimed that he'd found Weir that way and fled from Ser Denys in case he was the one who'd killed the man.

It looked like Weir would go free until Ser Denys made a mental leap. The recruit was thrown from the top of the wall the next morning, as he was judged unworthy even of hanging.

Where was the weapon?

Solution on page 211

# THE LATE ARMEN

**B**usy reading *The Dance of the Dragons*, Armen the acolyte lost track of time. When he came to his senses, the thought that he might be late getting to the Quill and Tankard filled him with significant distress. When he'd started reading, he had lit a pair of candles of identical heights but different widths. One had a four-hour lifespan, the other five hours. Now, the stub of the bigger candle was precisely four times the length of the smaller.

How long has he been reading?

Solution on page 211

# LYESSA

"**S**er Lothar." Ser Damon nodded politely to the steward. "Are you well?"

"Well enough," Lothar replied. "Although my cousin Lyessa has just been spent the last week under the care of a maester."

Ser Damon put some effort into looking interested. "Oh?"

"Well, there was nothing wrong with her whatsoever. No sickness, no injuries, no odd pains, nothing. Not a word of complaint from her either, not before, during or after. Still, the maester kept her abed for the whole time. He wouldn't let her do a thing for herself, not even touch a fork. Even after they let her go, she had to be carried away from them bodily."

"That does sound very odd," Ser Damon agreed.

"Nothing odd about it in the slightest," Lothar replied, and clumped off chuckling to himself.

Solution on page 212

# A HUNT FOR WORDS V

```
S U G A D A K H A K I L E K I
O T N O O S P T U O Y T E L Q
R H O M W A B Y E L R X R B D
R O R U Y E U B A E L I S H N
O R L N T G R L B N W E L L S
W S E D N D L O R E G S N M D
S E V A W E H T F O Y D A L N
C L H U A L C G C R C N A A A
N A K D L I Z A R D N B I Y I
E E N E T T L E S I I L U R R
G N M K A R H G N H U U Q O D
A A L B E T T G C G Q U O M A
H E N O O R H R O D E R I C K
R E T H G U A D N E K N U R D
J S I G F R Y D N P I N R U T
```

ADAKHAKILEKI
ADRIAN
ALBETT
ANGUY
ARCHIBALD
BAELISH
CANKER
DAELLA
DOQUU
DRUNKEN DAUGHTER
ELAENA
ELRON
GEROLD
GOWER

GULIAN
HAGEN
HAMELL
HOBERT
HULLEN
KEATH
LADY OF THE WAVES
LIZARD
MANNING
MORYA
MUNDA
NETTLES
OLENE
PAYNE

QUEEN
QUINCY
RODERICK
ROONE
SIGFRYD
SORROW
STOUT
SWEET
THERRY
TURNIP
UTHOR
WELLS

Solution on page 213

# SILVERHILL

**L**ord Anders Serrett found himself in a rather unusual position one day. Two days before, he had been 35 years of age but he was forced to concede that the following year, he would become 38.
"I Have No Rival", indeed.

How?

vieillesse

# FUSSY EATERS

Three-Fingered Hobb was called on late one evening to provide food for eleven unexpected visitors to Castle Black. Looking around the kitchens, he managed to find four portions of Hunter's Pie and four honeyed venison pasties. For the remaining three, the best he could do was bread and dripping.

He brought the food out the mess hall only to discover that five of the newcomers, for assorted reasons, would not eat the venison pasty and four more would not eat the Hunter's Pie. The remaining two were happy to eat either.

How many different ways can Hobb serve up the food?

# RAVENS

"You see, Gormon, if we state that all true ravens are black, then anything that is not black cannot be a raven."

"What about albino ravens?"

"Let us pretend, for this discussion, that they don't exist."

"Very well."

"So then, this green apple supports the theory that all ravens are black."

"That's ridiculous."

Is it?

Solution on page 216

# BLACKWATER

I'm generally found in wood,

And I'm at anyone's command.

I often do more hurt than good,

When I do get the upper hand.

I never fear the champion's frown,

Stout things I oftentimes have done —

Brave soldiers I have oft laid down,

I have no fear of sword and gun.

I always am in quietest repose,

But where I flow, much merriment ensues.

Who am I?

Solution on page 216

# A QUIZ OF ICE AND FIRE VI

1. What is Longclaw?

2. Which sword master is hired to teach Arya Stark to fight?

3. Which Grand Maester tended Jon Arryn in his final days?

4. Harry Lloyd, who plays Viserys Targaryen in the Game of Thrones TV show, is the descendent of which literary great?

5. Who orders the murder of Robert Baratheon's bastard children?

6. Who escapes Theon Greyjoy's clutches in Winterfell with Osha, Hodor, and Rickon Stark?

7. Where is the Milkwater?

8. What is a warg?

9. Who borrowed tens of millions in gold from the Iron Bank of Braavos?

10. Of where is Vayon Poole the steward?

Solution on page 217

# SER ROSBY

On the occasion of his daughter Melissa's 21st birthday, Ser Winton Rosby was called on to present his children to his ageing uncle, Ser Brandeth. He chose to do so from youngest to oldest, starting with little Leana and her brother Dale, who, as it happened, was exactly twice his little sister's age. When Jayne was introduced, her and Leana's ages combined then proved to be exactly twice that of Dale. Next was Gaweyn, who brought the total of the boys' ages to twice that of the girls' ages. Finally, Melissa's new age meant that the girls once again doubled the boys.

How old are the children?

Solution on page 218

# UNEXPECTED GOAT

**D**yre Den sits deep into Crackclaw Point, overlooking the sea. Its lord, Eustace Brune, is not known for his patience with fools. This left his groundsman, Nage, with something of a problem – what to do with an unexpected goat. In the end, he settled on pasturing it in a circular enclosure that had formerly been used as a horse corral before. Pushing thoughts of bulging eyes from his head, Nage tried to concentrate.

The goat needed no more than half the field for pasture, but goats were greedy. He decided to chain it up to the fence, with just enough slack on its chain to allow it access to half of the scrubby grass.

But should the chain reach to the midway point of the field, or should it be shorter, or longer?

Solution on page 219

# TRAVELLING LIGHT

**O**n the way to Maidenpool, via the Duskendale road, a group of travellers were pressing on past dusk to reach a particular inn. Their way was barred by a very rudimentary bridge, which would bear the weight of no more than two of their number at any one time.

While some of the four were sure-footed, others were extremely insecure, and they quickly realized that while Harra could cross in a minute, and Matt in two, Pate would need five minutes, and Myles a full ten minutes. To make matters worse, safe navigation required the use of a lantern and the group had but one between them, so some would have to cross in pairs in order to bring the lantern back to the remaining men. A pair, of course, would cross at the speed of the slowest man.

What is the least amount of time that the men could take to cross the bridge?

Solution on page 219

# LORDSPORT

"How many kills did you get yesterday, Rolf?"

"What's it to you?"

"Come on, man. Don't be shy."

"Pah. Figure it out for yourself. Take my tally and add two-thirds to it, then drag a third of those back off again and you'll end up at ten."

What is Rolf's tally?

## 89

# ANDA'S RULE

Ser Ferren, blessed by the gods, has an admirable 15 children, each born precisely 18 months apart. His eldest, Anda, prefers to say that she is seven times older again than her very youngest sibling, Jahn. How old is she?

Solution on page 220

# DRINKING WITH THIEVES

A precious cup that once belonged to Lady Alyce's grandmother had been stolen from the Graceford keep. Lady Alyce's captain, Obed Marsh, had narrowed the culprit down to one of five guards, who between them gave a web of highly contradictory statements. The key to finding the thief lay in the knowledge that two of the statements were false — but which two?

Einn: Mandrayke points the finger at me out of malice, for he is still angry about that thing with his sister.

Benfrit: Albar is a good man, and totally honest.

Mandrayke: Einn did it. He's total scum. He'd steal anything.

Albar: I've never stolen anything. I never will.

Boyard: You can rule Benfrit out. He's trustworthy.

Who is the thief?

Solution on page 221

# 91

# THE WULL

The Wull had 20 people in his household. Bread allocation for them was on the following basis – men got three loaves a day, women got two loaves and younger children half a loaf. Each day, the cook served out 20 loaves of bread for them. Assuming at least one of each, how many men, women and children were in the household?

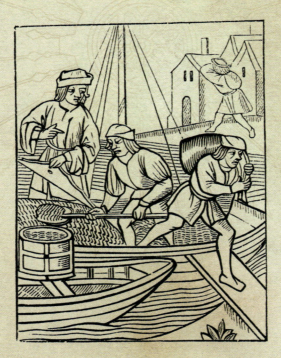

Solution on page 221

# HEATING UP

"It's getting warmer," Halder said.

Jeren nodded. "This is the fifth day in a row that has been warmer than the last. Multiply the five temperatures together and it comes to twelve."

Halder grunted. "That so?"

What are the temperatures of the last five days?

Solution on page 222

# A HUNT FOR WORDS VI

```
N M Y U R R A S N R O N G A R
O J R A S E P O N O D N O C Z
O S N S T Y G A I I A Y T S L
M T A O A A R K S R S L I A E
E H H G D R C E M M K L R P R
H U T N O Y N E A C E E E O R
T R E D W Y N E A N N A L S E
F G U L A S R L T C T K B M M
O O U F O D B S E N H S M U O
S O S V U E I H P Z E M U N L
E D A O L S T E E L N U H D D
T D A T T S A L Y S N P Q A T
A J T E L Y G L E Y L A N L O
G E R E W O T A L A D O R E W
K S O N O L A B R Y S N A T N
```

| | | |
|---|---|---|
| ALADORE | LANNA | SHELLA |
| ARMEN | LARENCE | SILENT SISTERS |
| BALON | LEYLA | STEEL |
| CONDON | MERREL | STYGAI |
| DAGON | NAERYS | SYLAS |
| DANOS | NOYNE | TANSY |
| DAVOS | OLDTOWN | THENN |
| DREAM | OSMUND | THURGOOD |
| ELLYN | QUENTEN | TOWER |
| ETHAN | RAGNOR | TYTOS |
| GATES OF THE MOON | RALPH | ULWYCK |
| HUMBLE | REDWYNE | URRAS |
| ISLES | RUFUS | |
| KETTLEBLACK | SARNE | |

Solution on page 223

# BLACK IRON

"You. Alleras. Are you paying attention, boy?"

"Of course, Maester Gormon."

"Is that so? Then tell me, why is a bird's egg the shape it is?"

What is the answer?

Solution on page 224

# FOUR STONES

Archmaester Mollos waved a bag around grandly before placing it on the bench and turning to the acolytes. "This bag holds four stones. Each may be black or white, but otherwise, they are indistinguishable. Now, say that I draw two white stones from it. Ponder, if you will, the chance of drawing a third white stone. If I were to tell you truthfully that there had been at least one white stone in the bag at the beginning, what effect would that have on the chance of drawing a third white stone that you just calculated?"

# A FOWL REQUEST

Ayoung septa was sent from her septry to the nearby city of Highgarden to purchase fowl for the order. Her superiors gave her 100 copper stars and wanted her to return with 100 assorted fowl, and no change.

At the market, she found that ducks cost two stars each, chickens were one star, pigeons were two to the star, ringdoves three to the star, and larks four to the star. Given that she had to buy at least one of each bird, how many did she come back with?

Solution on page 225

# A CURIOUS SPOT

**D**ragos Farrow turned to his father and pointed at a circular table in the corner of the room. "Father, do you see the spot on the edge of the table?"

Ser Richard looked up from his book. "Hmm? What of it?"

"Well, it's pointing into the corner, and it's eight inches from one wall and nine inches from the other."

Stifling a sigh, Ser Richard tried to look curious. "And so?"

"And so, I can work out how big the table is across."

Can you?

# A QUIZ OF ICE AND FIRE VII

1. Where are Daenerys Targaryen's dragons hatched?

2. What is Robb Stark's response to his sister Sansa's letter asking him to swear fealty to Joffrey Baratheon?

3. When Jon Snow leaves for the Wall, what gift does he give his sister Arya?

4. Who portrays Tywin Lannister in the Game of Thrones TV show?

5. Where does the warlock Pyat Pree stash the dragons he stole from Daenerys?

6. What weapon does Tyrion Lannister use against Stannis Baratheon's fleet?

7. What is the Harpy's Fingers?

8. After Ned Stark, who is the next Warden of the North?

9. What is the motto of House Tyrell?

10. Where is Oakenshield?

Solution on page 226

# STONE CROW

Torrek nudged Gunthor uneasily. "See that man by the other fire, the one in the wolf fur?"

"Of course."

"He's a stranger. What's he doing here?"

Gunthor laughed. "Going soft in the head, Torrek? His mother is my mother's mother-in-law."

"Eh?"

What relationship is the "stranger" to Gunthor?

Solution on page 227

## 100

# OLD HOGG

"Terrible fierce, the wildlings can be. They'll do dreadful things to a ranger, they will. Old Hogg the Hatchet was said to force a man to make a choice between terrible, terrible fates. Nasty ways to die. Stripped naked, soaked with water and tied up out in the snow, for one. Slowly impaled on a row of spikes. Thrown into a cage with a starveling wolf that has not been fed in six months."

"Well, I know which I'd choose, Boot."

How about you?

Solution on page 227

# FISHFOOT YARD

**W**alking through White Harbor, Davos Seaworth found a whole range of peculiarities in Fishfoot Yard, from terrible jugglers to a one-eyed hedge-witch with a nasty squint. The very strangest, however, was set up in front of Old Fishfoot, the square's resident merman statue.

A strange little man had arranged a tall board with a pulley at the top. A rope ran over the pulley. One end of the rope had a lump of stone tied to it. On the other end clung a villainous-looking monkey that clearly resented the bright red jacket it had been forced into. The man was keeping up a steady stream of extravagant prattle, encouraging people to place bets. He claimed that the stone and the monkey were the same weight and wanted bystanders to wager on whether the stone or the monkey would reach the pulley first, once he gave the signal for the monkey to start climbing.

Shaking his head, Ser Davos moved on. But which would reach the top first?

Solution on page 228

# BREATHING FIRE

My nose is long, my back is broad and round,

And in the cold, well then great use I'm found.

No load I carry yet I puff and blow,

As much as heavy loaded porters do.

What am I?

Solution on page 228

# A HUNT FOR WORDS VII

```
N H R P O D D I N G F I E L D
H N A Q I E N O K C I D J N S
C C E R O L L E Y B K O L Z S
R X T B M L N N N T J O I E L
Y Y R A A A R U N E A W T A A
B M O Y W M K E N B A R T H V
N D H A O S M C A W E A L R E
I N S R R E W N I L I Q E Y O
L O P D L A E O E R M N S N F
L M P C D N J Y D R D U I E R
U R E K A M N O R I T E S Y H
M O S T R A I T S I W S T R L
U G S E R A L A T H R E E B L
S I G R I N S H A R P G R T O
S O V A A R B P O L L I V E R
```

| | | |
|---|---|---|
| ARWOOD | IRON-MAKER | SHORTEAR |
| BARTH | JOJEN | SIGRIN |
| BAYARD | LITTLE SISTER | SLAVE OF RHLLOR |
| BRAAVOS | MULLIN | SMALL |
| BRYEN | NOLLA | STANE |
| BYRCH | PETYR | STRAITS |
| CLEMENT | PODDINGFIELD | TARLY |
| DELLA | POLLIVER | THREE |
| DICKON | REALM | TITUS |
| EDRICK | RHAEZN | UNWIN |
| ELEYNA | ROLLEY | WIDOW'S WATCH |
| ESTREN | SAWANE | WORLD |
| GORMOND | SERALA | |
| HARMA | SHARP | |

Solution on page 229

# A QUARTER AGE

**W**hen Gyles Grafton was born, his sister, Annami, was then a quarter of their mother's age and she is now a third of their father, Lord Gerrold's, age. Meanwhile, Gyles is now a quarter of their mother's age and in four years time, he'll be a quarter of his father's age. All of which served to thoroughly baffle Lord Robert Arryn, which was quite the point.

How old is Gyles?

# Winter

# WALKING THE WALK

**M**uch to the amusement of the Windblown, the Little Pigeon had a squared spiral path in his garden of contemplation. The path, one yard wide, formed a solid rectangle which spiralled in from its corner entrance to the very centre of the garden, a distance of 3,630 yards. The outside boundaries of the spiral were almost square, just half a yard longer than it was wide. If any of the Little Pigeon's men needed to speak to him, they were required to stalk the entire distance, winding slowly inwards, so to as not disturb his meditations.

How wide was the spiral?

Solution on page 230

# WILDFIRE

On patrol near the base of the Wall, Dalbridge spotted a wildling spy and immediately gave chase. The wildling had a 27 step advantage, and took eight steps for each of Dalbridge's five strides. However, just two of Dalbridge's strides were worth five of the spy's steps.

How many strides did it take Dalbridge to catch up with the spy?

Solution on page 231

# TROUBLE-IN-LAW

**D**orran Frey was trying to explain to an elder relative the assorted complexities of their relationship to each other. Gevin wasn't dealing well with the explanations however, and found the whole matter extremely confusing.

The trouble was that Gevin was, simultaneously, Dorran's father's brother-in-law, Dorran's brother's father-in-law and Dorran's father-in-law's brother.

How could such a thing have come about?

Solution on page 231

# A QUIZ OF ICE AND FIRE VIII

1.  Who is King Joffrey Baratheon's first Hand?

2.  How does Jon Snow kill the undead wight in Commander Mormont's quarters?

3.  Where does Walder Frey reside?

4.  Who portrays Tyrion Lannister in the *Game of Thrones* TV show?

5.  What is the name of Theon Greyjoy's father?

6.  How is Renly Baratheon killed?

7.  House Locke of Oldcastle can be found in which region?

8.  Who saves Daenerys Targaryen from death by manticore?

9.  Who does Edmure Tully marry?

10. To which house does the speaker of this quote belong: "Better to mock the game than to play and lose"?

Solution on page 232

# KING JOFFREY

"**I** want to kill you. You understand that, don't you?"

"Y-yes, my King. I'm –"

"Silence. My mother tells me I should be merciful. So I shall be merciful. If you can correctly predict your fate, without causing me confusion, then I will let you live, and if not, I will have you boiled."

Is there anything that the prisoner can say to avoid a horrible death?

Solution on page 233

# A GAME OF THROWS

Guard duty in Appleton was often relaxed and Giluan and his friend Argilac had invented a dice game to help while away the hours. Each man picked a pair of odd numbers between three and 17. Each number had to be different. They then took turns throwing three dice. The first man to total one of his numbers was the winner, unless the other could match a number of his own with one more throw, for a draw.

It should be obvious that the numbers they chose greatly impacted on their chances of victory, but are there two pairs of numbers that give both players identical chances of winning?

Solution on page 233

# THE RHOYNISH FASHION

**M**orreo was a quiet, peaceful sort, so it was something of a shock when he was found dead, in his home. The loss was worsened by the fact that he'd obviously been that way for some days. He wasn't old or injured in any way and he'd had no sickness or ailment. In fact, his death was accidental and could easily have been prevented with just a minor amount of outside assistance. It was quite odd, really. Although the weather was hot and dry – it had been for weeks, as was often the way in Sunspear – there was a small pool of fetid water by Morreo's side, about the size of his head.

What had happened to him?

la vieille

Solution on page 234

# A LOVER'S SIGN?

I am a wondrous creature,

To women a thing of desire; to neighbours serviceable.

I harm no house-dweller, except my slayer alone.

My stalk is erect and tall – I stand up in bed –

and shaggy down below (I won't say where).

Sometimes a countryman's comely daughter

will venture, proud girl, to get a grip on me.

She assaults my redness, plunders my head,

And fixes me in a tight place.

The one who afflicts me so, this woman with curly locks,

Will soon feel the effect of her encounter with me –

an eye will be wet.

Who am I?

Solution on page 234

# THE UPPER HAND?

Ser Harwood Stout and his cousin Ser Andros were playing dice. Because each round was short and they were evenly matched, they decided to play a series of 17 rounds, with the overall winner taking the pot. They were on the eleventh round when a messenger came from Lady Dustin, demanding that the men come to Barrow Hall.

Harwood was leading six to four, and felt that he should take the pot. Andros pointed out that the winner was the first to nine and he had plenty of time to overtake his cousin, so the pot should be shared equally. Harwood, however, felt that since he had the upper hand, this was unreasonable.

What is the fairest option, taking into account the matches unplayed?

Solution on page 235

# A HUNT FOR WORDS VIII

```
W  S  L  L  A  F  S  R  E  L  B  M  U  T  S
E  F  R  O  Y  C  E  C  R  O  S  L  I  N  E
L  O  M  M  Y  S  O  H  T  O  H  P  I  R  I
A  E  E  B  Y  M  T  U  S  K  S  W  R  P  K
E  F  K  L  A  F  T  W  R  R  T  E  R  Q  S
N  M  A  R  S  H  E  Z  O  T  G  A  G  H  E
O  L  E  N  Y  L  R  U  I  N  E  S  U  O  H
R  I  P  U  L  K  Q  C  I  D  O  S  L  R  T
D  E  R  F  M  U  K  R  G  X  O  T  A  I  F
O  N  E  T  O  L  B  E  B  O  U  R  C  N  O
O  A  L  D  E  T  N  A  R  B  O  R  E  H  D
L  J  D  R  H  E  V  B  D  R  E  D  Y  A  R
B  N  D  G  R  W  E  S  T  N  Q  C  W  X  O
H  T  I  A  V  R  N  E  G  E  A  H  M  I  L
J  L  L  U  T  Q  Q  E  V  X  G  T  I  B  N
```

| | | |
|---|---|---|
| ALYSE | LENYL | QHORIN |
| ARBOR | LIDDLE | RAYDER |
| BLOOD | LIGHTBRINGER | ROSLIN |
| COURTESAN | LOMMY | ROYCE |
| DOREA | LORD OF THE SKIES | RYKKER |
| DOUQUOR'S PIT | MAREI | TANDA |
| ERREG | MARSH | TICKLER |
| GENERAL | MHAEGEN | TUMBLER'S FALLS |
| GOODWIN | NOTCH | TUSKS |
| HOTHO | ORBERT | TWINS |
| HOUSE | OSWELL | UMFRED |
| JANEI | OTTER | VAITH |
| LACEY | PEAKE | |
| LAENOR | PRAED | |

Solution on page 236

# THE GOLDEN DRAGON

**M**erry Crane held a lively lunch party at the Golden Dragon, a sumptuous inn that nestled at the bottom of Rhaeny's Hill, near the Old Gate in King's Landing, in honour of a friend's birthday. It was a great success, and the final tally for food and drinks was 40 silver Moons. There were also 40 attendees, men, women and children, and all had a fine time. Given that the Golden Dragon billed three Moons per man, two Moons per woman, and one-third of a Moon per child, how many of each were in attendance?

Solution on page 237

# BEATEN DRUMM

"Captain Denys!"

"What is it, Tarb?"

"You said to split ten loaves amongst the ten prisoners, so that each man's share is one-eighth of a loaf less than the man before."

"And?"

"Well, Captain, I don't know where to start. What's the largest share?"

Solution on page 238

# SUDDEN DEATH

**A**waiting execution in the dungeons of the Rock, Byram tried to take some comfort from the sentence Lort Tywin had pronounced. "You'll die within a week, at midday, and you won't be expecting it."

Thinking it through, Byram realized that if he got to the seventh day, the execution would have to be that noon, so it would be no surprise. Which meant that the sixth day would be the last possible day. But that meant that if the executioner came on the sixth day, that too could be no surprise. In fact, by the same reasoning, none of the days were possible candidates.

Therefore, Byram was thoroughly astonished when the executioner killed him on the fourth day.

Where was the flaw in his logic?

# A QUIZ OF
# ICE AND FIRE IX

1. Where does Catelyn Stark have Tyrion Lannister arrested?

2. What trick does the Knight of Flowers use to beat Gregor The Mountain whilst jousting?

3. Who teaches Bran Stark the Dothraki art of horseback archery?

4. Lena Heady, who plays Cersei Lannister in the Game of Thrones TV show, played another strong mother in a TV sci-fi show. Who?

5. Which young prisoner is taken to Harrenhal with Gendry and Hot Pie?

6. Why does Tyrion Lannister imprison Maester Pycelle?

7. Who led the Greyjoy Rebellion?

8. What is the name of Davos Seaworth's third born son?

9. Who do the Brotherhood Without Banners sell to the Red Priestess, Melisandre?

10. What is The Merchant's Melancholy Daughter?

Solution on page 239

# LITTLE BOXES

"Master Terrence, Lord Robert wants something of you."

"Of course, Lord Baelish. How may I assist?"

"I'm glad you asked. He wants you to find pots of six different dyes and a stack of blank wooden dice, and see how many different possible arrangements of colours there are, if each die has its face dyed a different colour."

"I... what?"

"It's not difficult, lad. Two dice are effectively the same if you can rotate them so that each of their faces is in the same position. So if you use six dyes and keep to faces of one solid colour, there must be a limited number of different possibilities. Lord Robert wishes you to provide him with all these possible dice."

"That's utterly... No! Please, Lord Baelish, I hadn't finished. That's utterly, uh, understandable. I'll get to work."

How many different possibilities are there?

Solution on page 240

# THE FIGHT

The Brave Companions and the Golden Company fall at broadly opposite ends of the spectrum of sell-swords. The Golden Company are highly skilled, disciplined mercenaries who are famed for having never broken a contract, while the Brave Companions are a foul gaggle of criminals and outcasts whose one abiding virtue is their low cost.

The Golden Company found themselves storming a series of Brave Companion archery emplacements as part of a nasty ongoing conflict. Three members of Golden Company were sufficient to force any one emplacement to a stalemate. Four of them together would be able to overrun it in three minutes, five of them in two minutes and 15 seconds, and so on, with each additional man reducing the time proportionally.

On this occasion, there were four Brave Companion emplacements, and 13 members of the Golden Company. Assuming perfect tactics on the part of the Golden Company, who would win and how long would it take?

Solution on page 241

# NEEP

**I**'m a busy active creature,

Fashioned with a sportive nature,

I nimbly hop from tree to tree,

Under a well-wrought canopy.

I, to arms and blood a stranger,

Apprehensive of all danger,

Like the ant, for winter store,

Searching, treasures to explore.

Who am I?

Solution on page 242

# 122

# THREE STONE CROWS

Preparing for a salutary lesson, Archmaester Mollos prepares two bags. One holds a single stone, either black or white at equal chance. The other holds three stones, one white and two black. He adds a white stone to the first bag, shakes the two stones up and randomly draws a white stone back out.

Which of the following two options gives a better chance of pulling out a white stone – selecting one of the two bags by random coin-toss and blindly pulling a stone from it, or tipping both bags together into one bag and blindly pulling a stone from that combined lot?

Solution on page 242

# A HUNT FOR WORDS IX

```
N N R M J Q R H A E G A R E O
Y O E O T H E R Y S O V D U S
S M M P Y V G I L L Y L R Z A
E M L O C U N S L O A N E A L
Y E U E A L I A H G N B H L L
S N M T S T F R A W D E P A Y
G K A E T U S R N T E R E D D
D K D S E R T A N Y H O H Y A
O N O S R E N S A A W N S B N
R K O O L S I L Y W D R T R C
N C G M Y R L D J R L O A I E
A E L A R O F R K E D H E G R
A R A B O O G U N T H O R H D
A R D E C S T O N E S Q G T T
G E L Y K T R T T U J O S U A
```

| | | |
|---|---|---|
| AEGOR | GUNTHOR | RHAEGAR |
| ALGOOD | JOMMY | RONEL |
| ARWYN | JOSUA | SALLYDANCE |
| BERON | JYANNA | SARRA |
| CASTERLY ROCK | KYLEG | SELMY |
| CEDRA | LADYBRIGHT | SLOANE |
| DORNA | LAENA | STONES |
| DWARF | NAATH | THEODAN |
| EMMON | N'GHAI | ULMER |
| ERRECK | OBARA | VULTURE'S ROOST |
| FLINT'S FINGER | ORMOND | WYLIS |
| GILLY | OTHERYS | YOUNG |
| GODRY | POETESS | |
| GREAT SHEPHERD | QOHOR | |

Solution on page 243

# DARK HORSE

Deep in Crackclaw Point, Lord Eustace Brune found himself with a significant problem. The lands surrounding the Dyre Den had been savagely raided and the insult had to be answered. He rounded up a heavily-armed group, and set off on the raiders' trail, less than half an hour behind them. The hoofprints were clear in the soft ground and an hour later led the men straight to a cave, deep in the pinewood. Careful scouting revealed very sloppy defences, so Lord Brune and his men charged into the cave. It was wide, no more than 40 feet deep – and quite empty. There were signs of activity inside but a dozen men had ridden no more than 20 minutes ahead to the Dyre Den and then vanished, along with a quantity of livestock, two young women and their horses. There were no other exits, obvious or hidden. The walls, floor and roof were all solid. The men started muttering about sorcery and edged nervously back from the cave.

Can you think of a less supernatural explanation?

Solution on page 244

# CHAFF

In Oldtown, the three grades of corn – pure, fair and impure – are sold in baskets of different sizes. House Ambrose buys corn by the bushel. Two baskets of pure corn do not make a full bushel. Neither do three baskets of fair corn, nor four baskets of impure corn. However, add one basket of fair corn to two of pure, or one basket of impure to three of fair, or one basket of pure to four of impure, and in each of those cases, you would have a bushel.

What proportion of a bushel of corn does each grade's basket contain?

Solution on page 244

# THE STORMLANDS

In the Stormlands, Dunn the miller had two great friends named Dake and Cass. Dake's wife had died and his niece helped him around the house. Cass was also widowered and lived with his daughter. When Dunn got married, his new wife saw an opportunity to use more of the space they had so much of and to cut down on expenses at the same time, so, thinking about Dake and Cass, she suggested that everyone came to live in the millery. Dunn was only too happy to agree.

To keep everything fair, each person contributed 25 copper pence towards household costs. The first month's expenses came to 92 pence, so the remainder was shared out equally – returning each person an even number of pence, with nothing left over.

How much did each person receive, and why?

# MARIYA DARRY

Mariya Darry decided to host a gathering of her family, on both sides. To that end, she invited two grandparents, four parents, one mother-in-law, one father-in-law, two sisters, one brother, four children, two daughters, two sons, one daughter-in-law and three grandchildren.

What is the smallest possible number of guests?

Solution on page 245

# A QUIZ OF
# ICE AND FIRE X

1. Who warns Catelyn Stark about Cersei's murder of Jon Arryn?

2. How does Daenerys Targaryen receive her dragon eggs?

3. Which captured wildling becomes a servant in Winterfell?

4. Who does Sophie Turner play in the Game of Thrones TV show?

5. Where is Janos Slynt ordered after being removed as commander of the City Watch in King's Landing?

6. Which prostitute does Cersei Lannister kidnap to control her brother Tyrion's behaviour?

7. Who is Nymeria?

8. Which mercenary gives Daenerys Targaryen a pair of severed heads as a pledge of loyalty?

9. What is the Grey Worm?

10. Who was Mace Tyrell's father?

Solution on page 246

# MASTER WAYN

"Master Wayn, I am inclined to lock you in the dungeons for a long time indeed, but I admit that you have been dutiful in the past and you do have your supporters, so I will leave your fate in the hands of the gods." Ser Antarios looked suitably solemn but a tell-tale vein was throbbing in his forehead. He held up a bag and showed it to the assembled courtiers. "Inside this bag, I have placed one black stone and one white one. Pick the white stone and you may go free. Pick the black and your punishment will be… severe." He held out the bag.

Before his head was wrenched to the side by a zealous guard, Wayn got a quick glimpse into the bag. Both stones were black! He tried to speak, but the guard was holding his mouth shut.

"Pick a stone, Master Wayn," said Ser Antarios.

What can Wayn do?

# LORD OF LIGHT

Oro Tendryis was very particular about his surroundings, so when he had a room built for relaxation, he specified every detail – even that the window be perfectly square and five feet in height. When the room was finished, he inspected it and then called the builder back. He instructed the poor man, in no uncertain terms, that the window had to be altered to admit half as much light, without curtain, shade, shutter, a change in glass, or any other such impediment to a clear view. In fact, he further insisted that the window had to remain square and five feet in height.

The builder did eventually come up with a way to obey.

What was it?

Solution on page 247

# TALLHART

After the fall of the North, Bronn Tallhart was found dead in his chambers at Torrhen's Square. At first glance it looked like a suicide, for the room was barred from the inside with the key turned in the lock. When the door was battered down, Bronn was found in a heavy nightgown, hanging from a rafter by a short cord. However, there was no furniture in the room whatsoever and the man's booted feet were a good half-yard clear of the damp, musty floor. With nothing to stand upon, he simply could not have taken his own life. There appeared to be no other way in or out of the room, not even a window.

Ruling out sorcery, what could have happened?

# THE MELDING

**T**wo bodies have I,

Though both joined in one.

The stiller I stand,

The faster I run.

What am I?

Solution on page 248

# MASTER OF COIN

Three friends in a marketplace in King's Landing happened upon a purse, with money still in it. After checking out their discovery, the first man said to the second, "If I took this, I'd have twice as many copper Stars on me as you do." The second said, to the third, "And if I took it, I'd have three times as much as you." The third turned to the first in turn, and said, "If I took it, I'd have four times what you have."

What is the least amount of money in the purse?

Solution on page 249

# SER GARTH

Ser Garth Greenfield presented his sons with a large bag of shelled nuts and suggested that they share them out equitably. After a little thought, the children decided to split the nuts in line with their ages, which came to 17.5 years in total. The pattern they settled on was this: for every four nuts Lucion took, Rolan would take three and for each six nuts Lucion took, Criston would claim seven. Given that there were 770 nuts in the bag in total, how many did each boy get, and how old was he?

Solution on page 250

# CORDWAYNER

House Cordwayner of Hammerhal is known for its clever daughters. When their ages are taken together, Marisa and Alix Cordwayner total 44 years. Now, Marisa is twice as old as Alix was when Marisa was half as old as Alix will be when Alix is three times as old as Marisa was when Marisa was three times as old as Alix.

How old is Marisa?

Solution on page 251

# A HUNT FOR WORDS X

```
M A R G O T F R A N K L Y N K
N E Q E P S Z L E W Y S A B E
O M C I R E M O D O H F B N N
I O A E Y S O S F R Y D N A B
R N W E E G T N I R R A P S D
Y O S F K A H O O L I R Q T N
T O Y Y E A E Y N R V K U Y U
R J R D Y R R A A E R E O O M
D R M D R H R V W L H U R R R
E O Q R I A H E A U L E T E O
N R G A E R O E T D S E D N N
T A R G A R Y E N W N P X G Y
W D O A E A N A Y O Z O I A E
C N G E H T E F G A R T H K L
K A S S K Y T E K A Y C E R E
```

AEGON
AEMON
ANDAR
ARIANNE
AXELL
BANDY
CRONE
DARKE
DOGGETT
DOMERIC
ERRYK
EYRIE
FERRET
FRANKLYN

GARTH
HARRA
KAYCE
LEWYS
MAEKAR
MARGOT
MOTHER RHOYNE
NORMUND
OSFRYD
QUORT
RHONDA
ROSEY
SEAGARD
SILVER

SKYTE
SPARR
SPIKE
STAEDMON
STONE HEDGE
SWYFT
TARGARYEN
TOWERS
TYRION
URRON
VAYON
YOREN

Solution on page 252

# GEOR & ADRIC

Adric and Geor Dalt were cousins, and frequently caroused together – as much as Lemonwood allow, anyway. One evening, they met at an inn they often drank at and shared some spiced wine. An hour later, Adric was dead, poisoned, and only sheer fortune had kept Geor from similar death. In the days that followed, Geor had difficulty understanding why he had been utterly unaffected by the poison, while his cousin had been taken so swiftly. The two were very similar, with the same types of physique. Both had been healthy, ate similar foods and even had similar degrees of resilience, both acquired and innate. They had even drunk the same amount of wine. The only real difference that evening had been that Geor had been thirsty when they met, while Adric had not.

Why would that make a difference?

Solution on page 253

# RODRIK HARLAW

**R**odrik Harlaw decided to allow two of his captains, Myre and Kenning, to settle one of their periodic disputes with a race from Harlaw to Old Wyk and back. This was no ordinary race, however – the owner of the first ship back would lose.

That declaration left everyone speechless and old Volmark started kicking up a storm about month-long races of stubbornness, and men running out of water, and such forth. Rodrick shut off the entire debate with two simple words, and in doing so, ensured an extremely competitive race.

What did he say?

Solution on page 253

# MARRY A NAATHI

A Naathi chieftain had 100 daughters and gave any man a chance of marrying one of them. There was a trial involved, however. Having proved his mettle in several tests of skill, the suitor was shown to a pleasant room and introduced to each daughter, in no particular order. As she was introduced, he was also told the size of her dowry. He then had to immediately say "yes" or "no", with that decision being final. However, the marriage would only be permitted to go through if he somehow picked the daughter with the largest dowry of them all.

Is there a way to maximize the chance of picking the correct daughter?

## 140

# ARCHMAESTER MOLLOS'S CHALLENGE

"**D**o you think you are ready to claim the Red Gold link, acolyte? Very well then – correctly fill in the gaps in this piece of parchment using standard decimal digits from one to nine, so that each statement is true and accurate."

Below this line of text, and above the line of text that reads "The end", there are, in total:

\_\_\_\_ instance/s of the number 1;

\_\_\_\_ instance/s of the number 2;

\_\_\_\_ instance/s of the number 3;

\_\_\_\_ instance/s of the number 4; and

\_\_\_\_ instance/s of the number 5.

The end.

Solution on page 255

# Answers

# KIRRA'S APPLES

"A number plus its quarter" indicates that $5/4$ of the solution equals 15, so the answer is 15 x $4/5$, or 12 barrels.

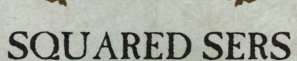

# SQUARED SERS

Ser Manfryd is 39, his wife is 34, his son is 14 and his daughter is 13. Ser Raynard is 42, his wife is 40, his son is 10 and his daughter is eight.

# FOWLER PLAY

If one is lying, the other must also be lying. Jeyne is on the right, and Jennelyn on the left.

# OLD WYK

The trick is to empty the central cell of each row. Nine acolytes can then be split between the corner cells at the end of that row however you please – so long as the parallel row has its corner cells filled in the opposite manner. So you could arrange, say, nine acolytes at top left and none at top right, then none again at bottom left and nine at bottom right.

# THE MAESTER'S HAND

In part, the air actually is cooler when blown quickly, because expanding from the tight stream you force it into reduces its temperature a little. Mainly however, a stream of air evaporates moisture from your skin, cooling it, and this effect happens more swiftly when the air is moving faster.

# DRAGONSTONE

Two widows married each others' sons, and each new union
brought forth a daughter. These six lie inside.

# A QUIZ OF
# ICE AND FIRE I

1. Theon Greyjoy

2. Tysha

3. Ser Jorah Mormont

4. With onions and salt fish

5. Daenerys Targaryen

6. Riverrun

7. Tyrion Lannister

8. Sandor the Hound

9. Lannister

10. Jaqen H'ghar

# LORD DAERON VAITH

If Gage is telling the truth, then Rafe also has to be telling the truth, and he claims Gage is lying, so it can't be him. If Rafe is telling the truth, then Gage is also telling the truth, so again, it can't be him. So Alarn has to be telling the truth.

# VARYS

A mole.

# FAIRMARKET

A hundred bushels of barley with 8 percent chaff is 92 bushels of pure barley. To sift 92 bushels of pure barley from a mix that was one-third chaff, you'd need half as much chaff as there was pure barley (two-thirds to one-third), or 138 bushels.

# HOUSE MARTELL

They are four generations of the same family, father to son. Petyr is Harlen's father. Harlen is Theodore's father. Theodore is Selmont's father.

# THE BAY OF CRABS

As the last quarter equals the third quarter, and the last half equals the first half, then the runners hit the three-quarter mark exactly three-quarters of the way through the race.
6.75 ÷ 3 = 2.25, and 2.25 x 4 = 9 minutes.

# A HUNT FOR WORDS I

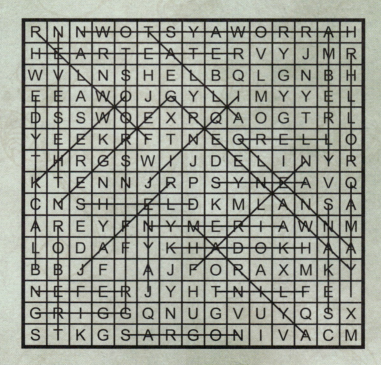

# DORNISH TROUBLE

It (obviously) takes one hour to travel ten miles at 10mph, and two-thirds of an hour to travel ten miles at 15mph. We need a distance that gives a two-hour gap between the two speeds. The difference for ten miles between the two speeds is a third of an hour, so we need six lots of that difference, or 60 miles. Sixty miles is six hours at 10mph, and that's an hour too late, so sunset is five hours away. That means the speed required to travel 60 miles in five hours is $60 \div 5 = 12$mph.

# CHICKENS

If 'x' is the number of buyers, 9x is 11 too much, and 6x is 16 too little. Looking at the difference, that means $3x = 27$, so x, the number of buyers, is 9. We know the value is 11 less than 9 times x, so the value is 81-11. There are nine men, paying 70 pennies between them.

# FIRST IMPRESSIONS

Dragons – take the first letter of each line.

# A LESSON OVER DINNER

If you approach this puzzle methodically, it's actually quite straightforward. First, you need to work out the size of the gap between shares that gives you the right ratio of $(A + B + C) \div 7 = (D + E)$. First, try it with just sequential numbers. $(5 + 4 + 3) \div 7 = 1.71$, which is 1.29 away from $(2 + 1) = 3$. Fine. Now try a simple increase in the sequence gaps. $(9 + 7 + 5) \div 7 = 3$, which is one away from $(3 + 1) = 4$. That's good, we've gotten $\frac{2}{7}$ closer to a difference of zero by increasing the gap between numbers by one. The difference is one, or $\frac{7}{7}$, so we try increasing the gap between numbers by 3.5 ($\frac{7}{2}$), to 5.5. This gives us 1, 6.5, 12, 17.5 and 23. $1 + 6.5 = 7.5$; and $12 + 17.5 + 23 = 52.5$, where $52.5 \div 7 = 7.5$. That's the right ratio. The five numbers together total up to 60 though, not 100, so we need to multiply our numbers by $100 \div 60$, or 1.667. So, our final breakdown of shares, from largest to smallest, is 38.33 spoons, 29.17 spoons, 20 spoons, 10.83 spoons and 1.67 spoons, where $(38.33 + 29.17 + 20) = 87.5$, and $(87.5/7) = (10.83 + 1.67) = 12.5$, and $87.5 + 12.5 = 100$.

This method of solving problems by putting in a series of wrong solutions and seeing how the answer changes is known as *Regula Falsi*.

# FREY TIME

Arwyn was being used to stand in for one of her cousins, who had been carrying on a relationship with the supposed lunatic. Her parents, disapproving of their love, had locked their daughter in the forbidden wing and made Arwen up to look like her. They then feigned cheerful family life as a charade for the suitor, to try to convince him that their daughter had forgotten him entirely and was carrying on with life as usual without him. It didn't work, so they gave up and sent Arwyn home.

# LISKER'S TASK

Indeed it is. Fifteen novices means Lisker plus 14 others, so there's enough people for him to work with two others each hour without repeating.

# THUNDERFIST

His age – the total of his sons and grandsons – has to be a square number if each son has as many brothers as sons. 64 is the only square number between 50 and 80.

# A QUIZ OF
# ICE AND FIRE II

1. Steward to the Lord Commander

2. Alliser Thorne

3. Because her sister's direwolf ran away after biting Joffrey Baratheon

4. Jason Momoa

5. Qarth

6. The Sea Bitch

7. Lord (Leyton) Hightower

8. His daughter, Cersei

9. Ramsay Snow, the Bastard of Bolton

10. Sandor Clegane, The Hound

# DAENERYS'S TEA

The tea was exactly as sweet as it was before.

---

# DAYNE'S PARADOX

There are a couple of common "solutions" to the Liars Paradox. Ser Dayne can be lying without that proving that all Dornishmen are liars. Say, for example, he lies, but his mother is scrupulously honest. Then he's simply lying and there's no paradox. Similarly, there would be no reason to assume every Dornishman lies all the time, so again, Ser Dayne's lie does not prove anything. For an alternative approach, he may simply be wrong about the matter, and so telling an incorrect "truth".

# THE SPRAWLING

A rose.

# A CAUTIOUS PACE

Because Thoros spends less time travelling at a higher speed, the average is not midway between the two speeds. Let's say it's a 24-mile journey. Then, at 4mph, it will take six hours there. Similarly, at 6mph, returning will take four hours. So Thoros will have travelled 24 x 2 = 48 miles in exactly ten hours. 48 ÷ 10 = 4.8mph. This average will be the same for any distance.

# A MATTER OF BIRTHDAYS

Because the number of links between people increases very swiftly as group size grows, in fact there is slightly better than a 50 percent chance that any two people in a group of 23 will have the same birthday. (To be exact, it is 50.7 percent, and you get a 99 percent chance with a group of 57 people).

# A HUNT FOR WORDS II

```
M R Q A J B B A R C E L Z G R
L S R E W O T E E R H T N O F
E S H A D D N M A H O O Y Y F
N A G G S E N O T S I R T L S
N R Y M I R H N S A P R G E E
O Y E G E A M D R Q L H R E A
D A M M E J H A I R Y E S T S
C W K B A T H Q F X N N A S M
S A Y L E N R A A A S S N Q O
R A V G O A B Y H F O S V O K
J Y R E V O C O O A C Q I R E
N L L Y D N A R N L U U L G G
W I L L E M L E K Y L A R Y S
R O N I L E A Q C S X R L L M
F I J Y Y U U X J E C E X E V
```

# AGE OF AMBROSE

If they are going to be 64 in seven years, then their current total age is 50. If her current age is twice her previous age, then his current age has to be three times her previous age (because it's twice her previous age, plus her previous age again). So he is 30, and she is 20, and when he was 20, she was ten.

# THE MALLISTERS

When you add complimentary numbers together – such as 12 + 21 – you always get a multiple of 11. The smallest gap between such numbers is nine, when the two digits of the numbers are sequential, again as in 12 and 21. 9 x 11 gives 99, and the only pair of numbers that fit the pattern and total 99 are 45 and 54, which are the ages of Alys and Jason Mallister respectively.

# TANNER

No. Provided that the rod is smaller than the tub – which it has to be to fit inside – there will always be a height beyond which the acid will not rise. This will vary according to the diameter of the tub and the rod, but it can certainly be calculated in advance.

---

# THREE BOXES

The answer is ⅔. Intuitively, most people feel that the box was either G/S or G/G, which means there is either G or S left, so the answer is ½. However, you have twice as much chance to pick a first gold coin from the G1/G2 box as you do from the G/S box, so the fact that you've already picked a gold coin means it's more likely that you have the G1/G2 box selected than the G/S box. Mathematically, you have three possibilities that start with a gold coin being selected – pick G, leaving S; or pick G1, leaving G2; or pick G2, leaving G1. Two of those three possibilities end with a second gold coin.

# SER GLADDEN

Let's call Gladden's current age "x".
Mathematically, his statement breaks down to $(x + 6) = (x - 4) \times \frac{5}{4}$. Multiply both sides by four to get rid of the divisor, so $4x + 24 = (x-4) \times 5 = 5x-20$. Now add that 20 to both sides. $4x + 44 = 5x$. Finally, subtract the $4x$ from both sides, and $44 = x$. Ser Gladden is 44, and in six years time, he'd be 50, which is one and a quarter times 40, his age four years ago.

# THE WOODSMAN

Crom is tanned, but if he had shaved off a huge beard a few days before, his cheeks, neck and jaw would be significantly paler than the rest of him.

# SIX BARRELS

We know that we need to add all the barrels to a total divisible by three with one left over. The total of all six is 119. That's not divisible by three, so removing 15 or 18 would be no help. Further more, 119 is two above 117, the previous number divisible by three, so subtracting a number that is just one above being divisible by three – i.e. 31, 19 and 16 – is also no use. The only barrel that is two numbers above a multiple of three is 20, so that is the beer. Remove that and you have 99 left, divided into 66 to one man and 33 to the other.

---

# GERIS CHARLTON

Geris does. He has two brothers and four sisters, while Leystone has one brother and three sisters.

# A TRAY OF CAKES

One trial is sufficient if each type is in the wrong position. Consider the cakes as A, B and C. If type C is in position A, then since position B cannot hold type B, it must hold type A, leaving the missing type B in position C. Similar logic holds for B being in place A.

---

# BUTTERWELL

According to the described relationship, Shay's great-grandmother was the sister of Perla's great-great-grandmother. Perla's grandmother and Shay's mother were thus second cousins, as their grandmothers were sisters. This means that Perla's grandmother would be second cousin twice removed to Shay's son.

# INFINITE REALMS

It's a trick question. As it turns out, the term "larger" is mostly meaningless when you start working with infinity. On the one hand, there are obviously twice as many whole numbers as there are even whole numbers. On the other hand, two things which extend to infinity are both the same size – infinite. With all that said though, modern science generally considers the two to be the same order of magnitude (known as Aleph Zero), even though their precise sizes are considered incalculable. We don't have room here, but check out the work of the mathematician Georg Cantor for a look at how startlingly beautiful the mathematics of infinity can become.

# A QUIZ OF
# ICE AND FIRE III

1. He refuses to have Daenerys Targaryen assassinated

2. Lord Varys

3. It has three eyes

4. Lily Allen.

5. Sandor "the Hound" Clegane

6. Tywin Lannister

7. The High Septon

8. As a punishment for conducting unethical experiments on living subjects

9. He is executed by Robb Stark

10. A pirate ship

# DAARIO AND THE GREY WORM

The Grey Worm is correct. Although there are more possible routes to success from 18 tosses, these extra success routes are not quite sufficient to overcome the basic problem, which is that rolling three sixes from 18 is broadly similar to rolling one 6 from six tosses 3 times in a row. The actual chances of making the roll, if you are curious, are 0.66 for the six-toss roll, and 0.60 for the 18-toss roll.

# KHALEESI OF THORNS

4.5 miles. The difference between the speeds means the time is split 3:1 between slower and faster. 6hrs x ¾ = 4.5hrs at 1mph (and 1.5hrs at 3mph)

# A HUNT FOR WORDS III

```
M A E R I E S M A R W Y L L A
A X J D L T E K E L R U K A A
C C L D J V A R D I S N R N D
O Y J E G D U M E F K K Y O O
R X Y D S T E P C N U A W D O
N N Z N L R E B M O K I O H W
E D M U N D N L A N L Y L A N
E S V O B O M M U L P P L D O
T Y Z S D N N S F C L D   N R
A E N A R R K O U L A E W A Y
E L L O C K E L T O S Y R D
R E H T A E W Y R R E M E R B
G M S L T O R G O N A L Y U D
N E B B I K N Y W E L M C R P
N A M O W G N I P E E W F W K
```

# QARTH

⅐ is approximately 0.14285, so 19 is around 114.28 percent of the answer. 19 ÷ 114.285 x 100 gives a stack size of 16.625, but that knowledge didn't help Xaro any.

# TWO TWINS

A pair of scales.

# BRIDGER CERWYN

Consider x =3y, and x + 18 = 2y + 36. Therefore x = 2y + 36-18, or 2y + 18. As x = 3y, we know 3y = 2y + 18, or y = 18. Then, x has to be 54. Eighteen years ago, Bridger was 54 and Beedie 18; now they are 72 and 36.

# MEN WITHOUT HATS

There was. If Barth has hair, he is being observed by Mudge;
if he is bald, he is looking at Gergen.

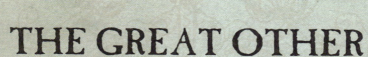

# THE GREAT OTHER

The maximum is 24, $3 + 5 + 7 + 9$. The minimum is 16, $7 + 9$,
for the nine who see through one eye can also double up as the
three blind in one eye and, because it doesn't say otherwise,
the five who see normally.

# VALAR MORGHULIS

We are told that the door and window were locked and sealed and that there was no other way in or out. With sorcery off the table, that means the murderer still has to be inside. Since there's nowhere to hide, the murderer must be in plain sight. Ser Normon had to have killed himself and staged the argument to make his family think he'd been murdered.

# PLAYING THE FIELD

To meet the conditions, the field will need to be 501,760 acres in size, with the fence having the same number of bars, and would be some 28 miles long on each side.

# ALLYCE & WILLIT

Willitt and Rolf were back-to-back.

# THE PLANK

Some of the wood is lost as sawdust, so each piece now weighs less than 2.5lb.

# LAZY LEO

The error is in thinking that the two situations, gain or lose, are directly comparable. They're entirely separate. The loss goes from two silver stags to one stag, and the gain goes from one stag to two stags, so the magnitudes are the same, and it's a flat 50/50 as to whether you gain or lose.

# A HUNDRED GEMS

Taking the most expensive first, 19 camels will cost 95 opals.
One ass will bring that to 20 animals for 96 opals. Finally,
the remaining four opals buy 80 goats, taking us to 100 opals
exchanged for 100 animals.

---

# PEARLS OF WISDOM

The second bag has a better chance, two-thirds, of holding a pearl.
The first bag has just a flat one-half chance.

# A QUIZ OF
# ICE AND FIRE IV

1. The King in the North

2. Robert Baratheon's will

3. Winterfell

4. Petyr "Littlefinger" Baelish

5. King-Beyond-the-Wall

6. Stannis Baratheon

7. The Free City of Myr

8. Her largest dragon

9. The Blackfish

10. Jaime Lannister

# AS THE RAVEN FLIES

Draw a perpendicular line from Cider Hall to the direct Longtable-Ashford road, and call the spot where it hits that road 'X'. You then have two right-angled triangles, (a) Longtable-X-Cider Hall, and (b) Ashford-X-Cider Hall. Both A and B share a side of length 12, from Cider Hall to X. From Pythagoras's theorem, there are only two right-angled triangles that have one side of length 12 – so because Cider Hall is nearer Longtable than Ashford, (a) is 12, 9, 15 and (b) is 12, 16, 20. We know the indirect distance is 35, so that has to be the 15-length hypotenuse from (a) and the 20-length hypotenuse from (b). The two sides of length 12 are the distance between Cider Hall and the road. That means that the two sides forming the straight road Longtable-X and X-Ashford have to be the remaining 9 and 16. So it's 25 miles from Longtable to Ashford direct.

# GOLD AND GREEN

You need a pair of square numbers that total 100, and the square root of one has to be three-quarters of the square root of the other. There's only nine square numbers less than 100, with square roots 1–9. A moment's thought will reveal that the two which add to 100 are 36 and 64, and their square roots are six and eight, which fit.

# THE DAWN'S DELAY

Time.

# REDFORT

Mychel will be half his father's age in $70 \div 3 = 23$ years and four months, so $x + 23.33 = (y + 23.33) \div 2$, or $2x + 23.33 = y$. Additionally, from Lord Horton's first statement, $6x = y$. So $2x + 23.33 = 6x$, or $x = 23.33 \div 4$, and Mychel is five years and ten months old. That makes Lord Horton 35, and, subtracting knowns from 70, Lady Houtella 29 years and two months old.

# RAYDER'S TOWER

The series of moves to escape the tower is as follows: 1. Put bundle in at top. It drops to bottom. 2. Put Ynga in at top. She drops, raising the bundle. 3. Switch the bundle for Stig. He drops, raising Ynga. 4. Ynga gets out at top, Stig gets out at bottom. Put bundle in, dropping it to bottom. 5. Stig gets in with bundle at bottom. Val gets in at top, raising Stig and bundle. Stig gets out at top, Val gets out at bottom. 6. Repeat steps 1–4, except that the bundle starts already in the basket. Now Ynga is at the top. 7. Ynga gets in at top, raising bundle. She gets out at the bottom, joining the other two. The bundle, now unopposed, drops to the bottom as well.

# FAIR ISLE

Considering the requirements as simultaneous equations, you need to ensure that the nine terms spread across the five variable types sum to 18. You will find that there are eight possible ways to add nine multiples of 1, 2, 3, 4 and 0 to 18. From these eight options, there are three different ways to pick five unique sets. Labelling the casks from A = 4 gal to E = 0 gal, one brother has to have 3A + B + C + D + 3E casks. The other four brothers can have any two of the following three pairs:

(A + 3B + 2C + D + 2E and 2A + B + 2C + 3D + E),

(A + 3B + C + 3D + E and 2A + B + 3C + D + 2E), and

(A + 2B + 3C + 2D + E and 2A + 2B + C + 2D + 2E)

---

# LADIES, NOT IN WAITING

Twice as many again means three times the current total. For x and 3x to fall equal distances either side of ten, they have to be five and 15. So there are five ladies.

# SER ONDRE

Enrike cheated. There's no way you could go that distance through the desert under the noon sun with a single flask of water and still have water left to sweat out, no matter how well conditioned you were. He either found a lot of water en route, or cut a big chunk of the distance out.

# A HUNT FOR WORDS IV

# A FOOL'S GAME

To calculate a summed there-and-back distance for each node in the path, multiply out the number of nodes, x, by (x-1) – trips – and (2x-1) – odd number distances. Then divide by 3, for terms. 50 x 49 x 99 ÷ 3 gives you a total distance of 80,850 yards, which is well over 45 miles.

---

# BREA'S FEAST

One man can fill all four roles, given the right set of familial intermarriages.

# GOODBROOK

The stable master lends a horse of his own to the herd, to bring the total to 18. Then the eldest son gets 18 ÷ 2 = 9 horses, the middle son gets 18 ÷ 3 = 6, and the youngest son gets 18 ÷ 9 = 2. Since 9 + 6 + 2 = 17, that leaves the stable master's loan horse, which he reclaims.

# SIMEON STAR-EYES

Hang the hat on the arrow before firing. You may not hit the target, but you'll certainly shoot through the hat.

# BAQQ

There are three possible combinations of winning with just one dice $(\frac{1}{6} \times \frac{5}{6} \times \frac{5}{6}) \times 3 - \frac{75}{216}$. There are three possible combinations of winning with two dice $(\frac{1}{6} \times \frac{1}{6} \times \frac{5}{6}) \times 3 - \frac{15}{216}$, but these are worth double $- \frac{30}{216}$. There is obviously only one way of winning with all three dice $- \frac{1}{216}$ and this is worth triple $- \frac{3}{216}$. Combining these odds $(75 + 30 + 3) \div 216 - \frac{108}{216}$, or 0.5 - an even chance.

---

# THE DOOR'S GUARD

A key.

# A QUIZ OF
# ICE AND FIRE V

1. Molten gold poured over his head to kill him

2. To keep Joffrey under control

3. He was forced by his father on pain of death

4. Jon Snow

5. King's Landing

6. One of the rulers of Qarth

7. Dorne

8. Bran Stark, in the body of his direwolf, Summer

9. To burn him as a sacrifice

10. Flowers

# KILLJOY

On the journey there, the ship is travelling an equivalent rate to 16mph. On the journey back, it is going at 4mph. The average of the two is the ship's speed, 10mph. Twenty-four miles there and back is 48 miles, which at 10mph, is four hours and 48 minutes.

---

# GOLD HONORS

You can break the three statements down into simultaneous equations, so $T + 1 (N + D) \div 2 = 28$, $N + 2 (T + D) \div 3 = 28$, and $D + 3 (T + N) \div 4 = 28$. Multiplying out, these come down to: $2T + N + D = 56$; $2T + 3N + 2D = 84$; and $3T + 3N + 4D = 112$. Now, solve the simultaneous equations by substituting through and you'll find that T, Triorro, has 20 gold honors; N, Nassicho, has 12 gold honors; and D, Donnimo, has four gold honors.

# THE MUSTER

Look at multiples of the biggest number first. We know dividing by seven leaves two, so that could be 9, 16, 23, 30 or 37. Dividing by five leaves three, so consider 8, 13, 18, 23, 28, 33, etc. Twenty-three shows up on both lists and, sure enough, dividing by three leaves two. Ser Gregor has 23 men.

---

# SALTSPEAR

First of all, the trapper takes the drunk priest to the far side and leaves him there. Then he takes the dog to the far side and returns with the drunkard. He then swaps the drunkard for the wine and takes the wine to the far side, with the dog. Finally, he returns empty-handed and takes the drunkard across.

# A RANGER'S DEATH

It melted. Weir stabbed Hale with a spike of ice. By running from Ser Denys, he gave the ice enough time to melt in the corpse, so no weapon could be found.

---

# THE LATE ARMEN

The two candle lengths intersect in this way after three hours and 45 minutes. At that time, the four-hour candle has just $\frac{1}{16}$ of its length remaining, 15 minutes out of 240, and the five-hour candle has $\frac{1}{4}$ remaining, 75 minutes out of 300.

# LYESSA

Lothar's cousin is a newborn baby. Delivered early, she was
watched carefully for a week to make sure all was well, before she
and her mother were released from the maester's care.

# A HUNT FOR WORDS V

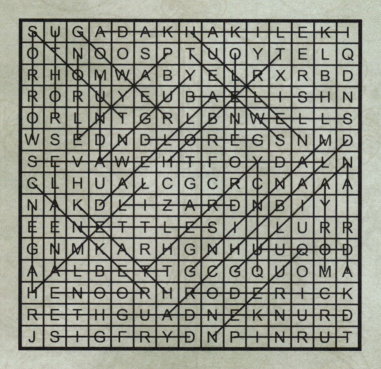

# SILVERHILL

Lord Anders was born on the last day of the year, and the day in question is the first day of the new year. Yesterday was his 36th birthday. At the end of this year, he will be 37. At the end of next year, he will therefore be 38.

Viellesse

# FUSSY EATERS

Assuming he doesn't just leave the food there in disgust and tell them to fight over it, we can break the visitors down as follows: five V, who won't eat venison pasty, 4 H who won't eat Hunter's Pie, and 2 O, omnivores.

All the possible options will fall into one the following categories:

(i) The four pasties feed all of H.

(ii) One O gets a pasty.

(iii) Both Os get pasties.

Permutation theory states that the number of options for selecting X items from a group of size Y is: $Y! \div (Y-X)!$ – where $Y!$ is all the numbers 1, 2, 3, ... Y all multiplied together.

In case (i), four pies (and three bread) are distributed amongst seven people. So selecting four from seven is $7! \div (7-4)!$, or $7 \times 6 \times 5 \times 4 = 840$. In case (ii), we have four pies going amongst six people, as well as three pasties amongst four. So that's $(6! \div 2!) \times (4! \div 1!) = 360 \times 24 = 8640$. In case (iii), four pies go to just five people, and two pasties go to four people. So $(5! \div 1!) \times (4! \div 2!) = 120 \times 12 = 1440$. Totalling all those options together, we have $840 + 8640 + 1440 = 10920$. The moral of this puzzle is simple: do not piss off your cook, for there are many ways to take vengeance.

# RAVENS

No, actually. The proof is not total – in fact, it's a tiny speck of supporting evidence – but the existence of a non-black non-raven does add some extra proof that anything non-black cannot be a raven.

# BLACKWATER

Ale.

# A QUIZ OF
# ICE AND FIRE VI

1. A sword

2. Syrio Forel

3. Pycelle

4. Charles Dickens

5. Joffrey Baratheon

6. Bran Stark

7. Beyond the Wall

8. A person who can enter into the minds of animals

9. Petyr Baelish

10. Winterfell

# SER ROSBY

Melissa, at 21, brings the girls' total from half to double that of the boys, so two-thirds of her age, 14, must be the boys' previous total, and the girls' previous total half that at 7, and the first score for the boys, Dale, must be 3 years and 6 months. So Leana is 1 year and 9 months, Jayne is 5 years and 3 months, Gaweyn is 10 years and 6 months, and we know Melissa is 21.

# UNEXPECTED GOAT

The chain needs to be longer than the radius. If it is equal to the radius, then the goat can reach midway at the centre, but the distance it gets will taper off as it goes above or below the midway line. If you're interested, the correct length for exactly 50 percent of the area would be 1.16 multiplied by the radius of the field.

---

# TRAVELLING LIGHT

Harra and Matt cross. Two minutes. Harra comes back with the lamp. Three minutes. Pate and Myles cross. 13 minutes. Matt comes back with the lamp. 15 minutes. Harra and Matt cross again. In total, 17 minutes. Note, Matt and Harra could return with the lamp in the other order without impacting total time.

# LORDSPORT

Look at the end first. Arriving at ten by removing one third means 15. X + ⅔ means 15 is ⅝ of X, so the tally is nine kills.

# ANDA'S RULE

Anda is 24. There are 14 lots of 1.5 years, or 21 years, between Anda and Jahn, and since she is seven times older again, her age has to be eight times his. So he is three and she is 24.

# DRINKING WITH THIEVES

The only self-consistent answer that identifies the thief is that Mandrayke and Boyard are the liars, and Benfrit is the thief.

# THE WULL

Consider upper bounds. Six men, one woman and one child would need too much food, so the maximum number of men is five. Similarly, eight women and 30 children are the maximums. By considering similar bounds for fixed numbers of men, the most expensive factor, you can quickly discover that one man, five women and 14 children together account for 20 loaves distributed across 20 people.

# HEATING UP

The temperatures are -2, -1, 1, 2 and 3. The number 12 is small enough that you need to get low-value numbers into the multiplication, and keeping the result positive means two negative numbers.

# A HUNT FOR WORDS VI

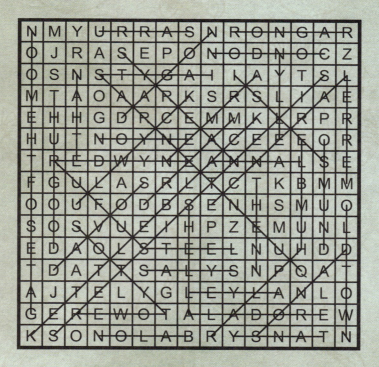

# BLACK IRON

So that if it rolls, it will roll in a circle, making it less likely to fall or be lost.

# FOUR STONES

Having one guaranteed white counter in the bag increases the chance of pulling a third white stone. Without the guarantee, all you can know is that there's a ½ chance that the next stone you pull will be white. With the guarantee, you can rule out four black stones as a possible starting state. That pushes the odds of drawing a third white stone up – to 7/12, to be precise.

# A FOWL REQUEST

There are in fact 2,678 correct solutions to this puzzle. One of them is 39 ducks, three chickens, nine pidgeons, 27 ringdoves and 22 larks, but it would be insane to list them all. We trust you. The point here is that some questions just don't have fixed answers.

---

# A CURIOUS SPOT

To find the solution, treat the problem as a quadratic equation. Double and then square root the product of the two distances. $9 \times 8 = 72 \times 2 = 144$, which is the square of 12. Likewise, sum the two distances, $9+8 = 17$. Then the radius of the table is either the difference or the sum of the two values. $17-12 = 5$ and $17 + 12 = 29$. Since the spot is on the near side of the table – it's pointing into the corner – the larger value is the correct radius and the table is 58 inches in diameter. If the spot had been on the far side, the table would have had to have been just ten inches in diameter.

# A QUIZ OF
# ICE AND FIRE VII

1. In her husband's funeral pyre

2. He declares war on the Lannisters

3. A sword

4. Charles Dance

5. The House of the Undying

6. Wildfire

7. A whip

8. Roose Bolton

9. "Growing Strong"

10. A fortress on the Wall

# STONE CROW

The stranger is Gunthor's uncle.

---

# OLD HOGG

After six months with no food, the wolf is going to be dead.

# FISHFOOT YARD

The stone will reach the pulley first – as long as the monkey pulls on the rope. The monkey will not be able to ascend the rope until the stone jams in the pulley at the top.

---

# BREATHING FIRE

A pair of bellows.

# A HUNT FOR WORDS VII

```
N H R P O D D I N G F I E L D
H N A Q I E N O K C I D J N S
C G E R O L L E Y B K O L Z S
R X T B M L N N N T J O E L
Y Y R A A A R U N E A W T A A
B M O Y W M K E M B A R T H V
N D H A O S M C A W E A L R E
N S R R E W N I X I Q E Y O
L O P D L A E Q E R M N S N F
L M P C D N J Y D R D U E R
U R E K A M M O R I T E S Y H
M O S T R A I T S I W S T R L
U G S E R A L A T H R E E B L
S I G R I N S H A R P G R T O
S O V A A R B P O L L I V E R
```

# A QUARTER AGE

Let's set some definitions. Mother's age when Gyles was born is M. Similarly, Annami's age was A when Gyles was born, and Father's age was F. Gyles was 0 when he was born (obviously), but his age now is X. Everyone's current age is X+ their age when Gyles was born.

So, we know from the question that:

$A = M \div 4$; $A+X = (F+X) \div 3$; $X = (M+X) \div 4$; and $X+4 = (F+X+4) \div 4$.

Now, multiply out all the fractions.

$4A = M$; $3A + 3X = F + X$; so $3A + 2X = F$; $4X = M + X$; so $3X = M$; and

$4X + 16 = F + X + 4$; so $3X + 12 = F$

That gives us two equations for M, and two for F, which we can combine.

$4A = 3X$; which solves to $4A \div 3 = X$; and

$3A + 2X = 3X + 12$; or, solving to leave just a number, $3A - X = 12$.

Now we can combine those two:

$3A - 4A \div 3 = 12$; which gives us $9A - 4A = 36$; $5A = 36$; $A = 36 \div 5 = 7.2$

So Annami was 7.2 yrs old when Giles was born. From that, everything else falls into place. X, Gyles age, = $4A \div 3$, or 9.6. Annami's current age is 7.2+9.6, or 16.8 years. Mother's age is 4X, or 38.4 years; and father's age = $4X + 12$, or 50.4 years.

---

# WALKING THE WALK

Since the spiral is one yard wide, its length equals the surface area of the garden. A rectangle's area is length x width, but since the two are very close to each other, the area is very close to being square. The nearest square number before 3630 is 3600, which is 60 x 60. Half of 60 is indeed 30, for the missing amount. So the path is 60 x 60.5 and the width, the lesser of the two, is 60 yards.

# WILDFIRE

Since the wildling has a 27-step headstart, when he has run 48 steps, he'll be 75 of his steps ahead of Dalbridge's starting position. During the same time, Dalbridge will take 30 strides – which, at 2.5:1, are worth 75 steps. So Dalbridge will catch the spy after 30 strides.

# TROUBLE-IN-LAW

In order for the relationship to hold, three separate familial interconnections are necessary. Dorran's father must have married Gevin's sister; Dorran's brother must have married Gevin's daughter; and Dorran's wife must have been Gevin's niece.

# A QUIZ OF
# ICE AND FIRE VIII

1. Tywin Lannister, his grandfather

2. With fire, in the form of a lit lantern

3. The Twins, a fortified bridge

4. Peter Dinklage

5. Balon

6. By Melisandre's sorcerous shadow assassin

7. The North

8. Barristan Selmy

9. Roslin Frey

10. House Lannister (the speaker is Genna)

# KING JOFFREY

If the prisoner says that he will be allowed to live, Joffrey can kill him to prove him wrong. If he says that he will be killed, and he is killed, then he predicted correctly and should have lived – save that if he had lived, he'd have predicted incorrectly. This is irreconcilable and certainly counts as due confusion, as per Joffrey's get-out clause. The best course is to turn the statement back on the king, saying, "I predict that if I can correctly predict my fate, without causing you confusion, then you will let me live, and if not, you will have me boiled." This statement is unarguably correct in all cases, provided that it is accepted as a valid prediction.

---

# A GAME OF THROWS

Yes, the numbers five and nine have a $^{31}/_{216}$ chance of winning, as do the numbers 13 and 15. There are 216 possibilities for three dice. From these, there are six ways of getting five, 25 ways of getting nine, 21 ways of getting 13, and ten ways of getting 15.

# THE RHOYNISH FASHION

Morreo was a pet fish, and his bowl had dried up in the heat.
No one thought to replenish his water.

la vieille

---

# A LOVER'S SIGN?

An onion.

# THE UPPER HAND?

The most equitable option is to work out the chance of each man winning, and divide the pot along those lines. As each game is $^{50}/_{50}$, and there are seven games to play, those seven games have 128 possible outcomes. Andros needs to win five games out of the last seven. From combinatorics, there are 29 outcomes where he wins five or more games, so his chance of victory is $^{29}/_{128}$, or 22.65 percent. Similarly, Harwood will win 99 times out of 128 from here, or 77.35 percent. So to be scrupulously fair, the pot should be split so give Harwood 77.35 percent of the total.

# A HUNT FOR WORDS VIII

| W | S | L | L | A | F | S | R | E | L | B | M | U | T | S |
| E | F | R | O | Y | G | E | C | R | O | S | L | I | N | E |
| L | O | M | M | Y | S | O | H | T | O | H | P | I | R | R |
| A | E | E | B | Y | M | T | U | S | K | S | W | R | P | K |
| E | F | K | L | A | F | T | W | R | R | T | E | R | Q | S |
| N | M | A | R | S | H | E | Z | O | T | G | A | G | H | E |
| O | L | E | N | K | L | R | U | I | N | K | S | U | O | H |
| R | I | P | U | L | K | Q | C | I | B | O | S | L | R | T |
| D | E | R | F | M | U | K | R | G | X | O | T | A | F |
| O | N | E | T | O | L | B | E | B | O | U | R | C | N | O |
| O | A | L | D | E | T | N | A | R | B | O | R | E | H | D |
| L | J | D | R | H | E | V | B | D | R | E | D | Y | A | R |
| B | N | D | G | R | W | E | S | T | N | Q | C | W | X | O |
| H | T | A | V | R | N | E | G | E | A | H | M | I | L |
| J | L | L | U | T | Q | Q | E | V | X | G | T | I | B | N |

# THE GOLDEN DRAGON

You have two simultaneous equations, which is enough to reduce the terms – children are the best bet to eliminate – and use some basic trial and error. $M + W + C = 40$, and $3M + 2W + C \div 3 = 40$. So $C \div 3 = 40 - 2W - 3M$, or $C = 120 - 6W - 9M$. Therefore $M + W + 120 - 6W - 9M = 40$, and reducing, $80 = 5W + 8M$. Looking at whole integer solutions to that indefinite equation, eight women and five men form a good place to start. Together, they would account for $16 + 15 = 31$ Moons, across 13 people. That leaves 27 children to bring the total to 40, costing nine Moons, to also bring the total to 40. So there were eight women, five men, and 27 children.

# BEATEN DRUMM

The portions must average out to a loaf each, and there are only nine differences between the ten shares. Take half of the intended difference – that's $\frac{1}{16}$ – and multiply it by the nine differences, which is $\frac{9}{16}$. Then add that median to the average share, and 1 and $\frac{9}{16}$, or 1.5625 loaves, is the largest share. (The smallest share, incidentally, is $\frac{7}{16}$).

# SUDDEN DEATH

The error lies in the assumption that once the seventh day has been ruled out, it stays ruled out. On day three, execution on days four through seven remain perfectly possible. In fact, Byram's logic only really amounts to, "I'll be killed some time next week" – not all that surprising.

# A QUIZ OF
# ICE AND FIRE IX

1. The Inn at the Crossroads

2. He rides a mare in heat

3. Maester Luwin

4. Sarah Connor

5. Arya Stark

6. Pycelle is a spy for Cersei Lannister

7. Balon Greyjoy

8. Matthos

9. Gendry

10. A play

# LITTLE BOXES

Consider the six dyes as A–F. Each die uses all six colours, so we need one colour as our point of origin for reference. Assume the A face is always rotated towards us. That leaves five options for the diametrically opposite face, and four further faces in a band around the middle. For any given opposite face (for example, F), the band will always have the same four colours, so assume one – say, B – is rotated to the top. Then there are three other colours to distribute, and they can be arranged in six ways. So we have 5 x 6 = 30 total variations.

# THE FIGHT

Initially, the Golden Company take on the emplacements three-to-one, with the 13th man helping one group to victory in 180 seconds. The four thus freed go on to split up again, so two emplacements are being worn down by four men, while five destroy a second emplacement in 135 seconds. During that 135 seconds, the groups of four will wear their emplacements down to 25 percent health. After that, the Golden Company split six and seven versus the two emplacements. Seven men would take an emplacement in 90 seconds, but the target has just 25 percent to go, so it's only 22.5 seconds. The six men who would win against a full emplacement in 108 seconds, have done a little over 20 percent more damage to their target. That leaves 5 percent to go against all 13 men, which will take about 2.5 seconds. So the total time required for the Golden Company to win is 340 seconds, a little under five-and-three-quarter minutes.

# NEEP

A squirrel.

# THREE STONE CROWS

The first bag has a ⅔ chance of holding a white stone, and the second has a ⅓ chance of you selecting the white at random. Since it's ⁵⁰⁄₅₀ as to which bag you get, the overall chance of pulling a white stone is 1/2. The combined bag contains either WWBB (⅔ chance) or WBBB (⅓ chance). WWBB would give you a 1/2 chance of pulling white, but WBBB would give only ¼, so between the two, there's only a ⁵⁄₁₂ chance of white. You'd do better selecting the coin-toss.

# A HUNT FOR WORDS IX

```
N N R M J Q R H A E G A R E O
X O E O T H E R Y S O V D U S
S M M P Y V G I L L Y L R Z A
E M L O C U N S L O A N E A L
Y E U E A L A H G N B H L L
S N M T S F R A W D E P A Y
G K A E T U S R N T E R E D D
D K D S E R T A N Y H O H Y A
O N O S R E N S A A W N S B N
R K O O L S L K W D R T R C
N C G M Y R L D J R L Q A E
A E L A P O F R K E D H E G R
A R A B O O G U N T H O R N D
A R D E C S T O N E S Q G T T
G E L Y K T R T T U J O S U A
```

# DARK HORSE

The raiders turned their horseshoes round to face the wrong way
before the raid. Brune and his men charged off back to the cave
that the raiders had used as a staging post.

# CHAFF

Since we have three conditions for making a full bushel, we
can use simultaneous equations to solve the problem. We know
that $2a + b = 1$, $3b + c = 1$ and $4c + a = 1$. From this, substitute
through to find that $a = \frac{9}{25}$, $b = \frac{7}{25}$, and $c = \frac{4}{25}$, where
A is pure, B is fair and C is impure.

# THE STORMLANDS

Cass's daughter, Dake's niece and Dunn's wife are all the same individual, so there are only four people involved. 100 pence collected with 92 spent leaves eight to be shared between the four, at two pence each.

# MARIYA DARRY

Just seven people can fill all those requirements – a married couple with their three children (two girls and a boy), and the husband's parents.

# A QUIZ OF
# ICE AND FIRE X

1. Her sister, Lysa

2. As a wedding gift

3. Osha

4. Sansa Stark

5. To join the Night Watch

6. Ros

7. Arya Stark's direwolf – or the legendary
queen she's named after

8. Daario Naharis

9. He is the leader of Daenerys's Unsullied warriors

10. Luthor

# MASTER WAYN

If both stones are black, then Wayn has to eliminate the one he picks – by throwing it away, or swallowing it, or some such. Then he can point to the bag to show the stone that he did not pick, which will be black. At that point, Antarios has to either let him go or admit that the trial was rigged.

# LORD OF LIGHT

The builder reconstructed the window as a square diamond – still five feet high, but by going from midpoint to midpoint of each original side, the diamond removed half of the light, effectively dividing the original square into quarters, and then halving each quarter.

# TALLHART

Bronn used a block of ice as a stand to get himself
in position, then kicked it over to kill himself.

# THE MELDING

An hourglass.

# MASTER OF COIN

Again, this a problem for simultaneous equations. The purse holds 23 Stars and, for the record, the men have nine Stars, 16 Stars and 13 Stars respectively.

# SER GARTH

For each 12 nuts Lucion gets, Rolan will get nine and Criston will get 14. Together, these amounts total 35. As 17.5 is half 35, the boys ages are half of the listed amounts of nuts in one cycle, so Lucion is six, Rolan is four-and-a-half, and Criston is seven. There are 22 lots of 35 in 770, so multiply the nuts per cycle by 22 to find the nut totals – 264, 198 and 308 respectively.

# CORDWAYNER

If you follow the logic through, Marisa's age must be one and two-thirds Alix's. Since they're 44 in total, Marisa is 27½, and Alix is 11 years younger, at 16½. Consider the original statement with the ages in question inserted, for clarity, working from the back: when Marisa was three times as old as Alix, Marisa was 16½ and Alix five-and-a-half. Then we get 49½ for the age Alix will be when she is three times as old as Marisa was then. When Marisa was half this she was 24¾. And at that time Alix must have been 13¾. Therefore Marisa is now twice as old, 27½, and Alix is 16½.

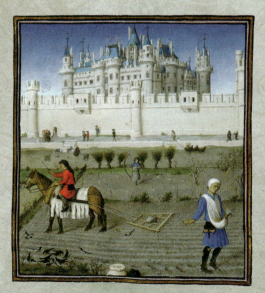

# A HUNT FOR WORDS X

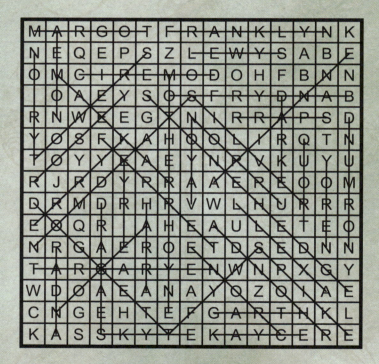

| M | A | R | G | O | T | F | R | A | N | K | L | Y | N | K |
|---|---|---|---|---|---|---|---|---|---|---|---|---|---|---|
| N | E | Q | E | P | S | Z | L | E | W | Y | S | A | B | E |
| O | M | G | I | R | E | M | O | D | O | H | F | B | N | N |
| I | O | A | E | Y | S | O | S | F | R | Y | D | N | A | B |
| R | N | W | E | E | G | N | I | R | R | A | P | S | D | D |
| Y | O | S | F | X | A | H | O | O | L | I | R | Q | T | N |
| T | O | Y | Y | R | A | E | Y | N | R | V | K | U | Y | U |
| R | J | R | D | Y | R | R | A | A | E | R | E | O | O | M |
| D | R | M | D | R | H | P | V | W | L | H | U | R | R | R |
| E | O | Q | R | I | A | H | E | A | U | L | E | T | E | O |
| N | R | G | A | E | R | O | E | T | D | S | E | D | N | N |
| T | A | R | G | A | R | Y | E | N | W | N | R | X | G | Y |
| W | D | O | A | E | A | N | A | Y | Q | Z | Q | I | A | E |
| C | N | G | E | H | T | E | F | G | A | R | T | H | K | L |
| K | A | S | S | K | Y | Y | E | K | A | Y | C | E | R | E |

# GEOR & ADRIC

The poison was in the spices and it took time to seep out into the wine. Geor, being thirsty, poured himself wine immediately and thus only got a tiny dose of poison. Adric was slower and by the time he poured his drink, it was already deadly.

# RODRIK HARLAW

*"Switch ships."*

# MARRY A NAATHI

The answer lies in Euler's Number, "e", the mathematical constant that (amongst other things) represents the ratio of growth of continual compound interest. The best chance of finding the right girl out of X is to reject all the girls up to the one in position $X \div e - 37$, for 100 girls – and then accept the next girl whose dowry is higher than all those given previously. This strategy gives, coincidentally, a 37 percent chance of picking the correct daughter.

# ARCHMAESTER MOLLOS'S CHALLENGE

There are 3 x 1, 2 x 2, 3 x 3, 1 x 4 and 1 x 5. With five example digits, and five spaces, the total number of the values you fill in must equal ten. To get started, try all ones. This is clearly wrong, but totalling them, this gives you 6 x 1, and one each of the other four. So plug that in and check again – 6 1 1 1 1. Still false; you now have 5 1 1 1 1. Keep on processing the numbers, and that gives you 5 1 1 1 2, which leads > 4 2 1 1 2 > 3 3 1 2 1, and finally > 3 2 3 1 1, which is correct.

# ACKNOWLEDGEMENTS

Illustrations supplied by the following sources: *120 Great Paintings from Medieval Illustrated Books*, edited by Carol Belanger Grafton; *Costume and Ornament of the Middle Ages in Full Color* by Henry Shaw; *Full Color Heraldic Designs* (Dover Books); *Full Color Medieval Ornament* (Dover Books); *Medieval Knights, Armor & Weapons* (Dover Books); *Renaissance & Medieval Costume* by Camille Bonnard; *Treasury of Medieval Illustrations* by Paul Lacroix